An MD Examines

AN M.D. EXAMINES

WHY DOESN'T GOD STOP EVIL?

DR. BRAD BURKE

Victor®
The Bible Teacher's Teacher

COOK COMMUNICATIONS MINISTRIES
Colorado Springs, Colorado • Paris, Ontario
KINGSWAY COMMUNICATIONS LTD
Eastbourne, England

Victor® is an imprint of
Cook Communications Ministries, Colorado Springs, CO 80918
Cook Communications, Paris, Ontario
Kingsway Communications, Eastbourne, England

WHY DOESN'T GOD STOP EVIL?

Published in association with the literary agency of Les Stobbe, 300
Doubleday Road, Tryon, NC 28782.

The Web addresses (URLs) recommended throughout this book are solely
offered as a resource to the reader. The citation of these Web sites does not
in any way imply an endorsement on the part of the author or the publisher,
nor does the author or publisher vouch for their content for the life of this
book.

Cover Design: Marks & Whetstone
Cover Photo Credit: © BigStockPhoto

First Printing, 2006
Printed in the United States of America

1 2 3 4 5 6 7 8 9 10 Printing/Year 10 09 08 07 06

ISBN-13: 978-0-7814-4281-7
ISBN-10: 0-7814-4281-8

LCCN: 2006923058

To my parents, David and Lucille,
who, by God's grace,
instilled within me a passion
for memorization and
meditation on Scripture

CONTENTS

ACKNOWLEDGMENTS

My second career as a writer unexpectedly began in my second year of medical school when I stumbled into the creative world of screenwriting. In a sense, An MD Examines came together remarkably like a major Hollywood film, complete with an executive producer, coproducers, editors, directors, a film studio, a screenwriter—even actors and actresses. Using the film analogy, here are the "rolling credits."

I must begin by thanking my Executive Producer on this extensive project, my Lord and heavenly Father. The astonishing way in which God brought all these talented individuals together blows the fuses in my mind. Whether or not this production wins an Oscar here on earth, God, and God alone, deserves all the glory.

Heather Gemmen, my brilliant producer and content editor, rocks! She enthusiastically presented this project to the studio, Cook Communications. My exceedingly wise coproducer, trusted friend, and mentor for more than twenty-five years, Garry Jenkins, helped steer me clear of false doctrine and "fluff."

ACKNOWLEDGMENTS

Craig Bubeck, like an experienced Tinseltown director, finely directed the thematic and visual components of this project at Cook. And the assistant director, Diane Gardner, and film publicist, Michele Tennesen, smoothly coordinated events, meetings, and communiqué between location shoots. There are so many others at Cook who played key roles; I thank them so much for their dedication to spreading God's truth around the world!

Every film needs a good editor. In addition to those mentioned above, Audrey Dorsch worked her own movie magic and brought the scenes together seamlessly.

Script consultants can make or break a film. Several provided valuable advice from scene one to "The End": Garry and Matt Jenkins, Sherri Spence, Dr. Val Jones, Wendy Elaine Nelles, and my parents. God provided other consultants for the production at key times, including world-renowned surgeon and author Dr. Paul Brand.

The Word Guild, the largest Christian writing association in Canada, played the role of a Hollywood talent agency perfectly, bringing together the screenwriter with the editors, producer, script consultant, agent, and even the production company for this powerful movie.

And what's a film without the actors and actresses? My sincere thanks also goes out to all those individuals who brought this film to life by allowing the world to see their inspiring stories.

I am grateful to Les Stobbe, my hardworking agent who helped make this series possible. My heartfelt appreciation also goes to my parents, David and Lucille, whose understanding and support during those tough years when I took a half-decade sabbatical from medicine to write this series ensured my success. I love them both very much.

In almost every film there is a love interest. To Erin, my beautiful wife, I'm looking forward to serving the Lord together for the rest of our lives.

And finally, to my brother Darryl (a stunt coordinator in training) who told me in 1999 that one day I would write a book—and I laughed …

I apologize.

Understanding God, for the dedicated and faithful believer, is a day-by-day, hour-by-hour, mind-, heart-, and soul-grappling journey, yielding priceless and unfathomable treasures ... sometimes by the minute ... sometimes when the saint is least expecting it....

A RÉSUMÉ UNLIKE ANY OTHER

What would you think if the following résumé came across your desk?

GOD

Address: Everywhere

Home Phone: Talk wherever you are; I'll hear you.

Birth Date: None (from all eternity)

SUMMARY OF QUALIFICATIONS:

Creation to present: Creator, Guardian, Judge, Father, Preserver, Shepherd, and Ruler. As the Potter, I am "fired" from my position by hundreds of thousands of clay pieces every day—but so far, no one has been able to find a decent replacement. I remain the altogether holy, sovereign, just, and powerful God of the universe.

EDUCATION:

None (Isa. 40:13–14)

WHY DOESN'T GOD STOP EVIL?

DEGREES:

BA, BS, BFA, BBA, BM, BMEd, BARC, EDS, EDD, MA, MAT, MPA, MFA, MSN, MM, MS, AB, MED, MSBA, MTX, ThM, ThD, DD, MPhil, MPH, DBA, MSW, DPharm, MOT, MPT, DPT, DDS, MPA, MDiv, PhD, MD, DO, JD, LLM, SJD, MBA, DMgt, DC, DVM. All summa cum laude. (More degrees available upon request.)

PROFESSIONAL EXPERIENCE:

I created the entire universe out of nothing (Gen. 1), including 150 billion galaxies, 1×10^{37} stars (a one with 37 zeroes behind it), 50 million animal species, and 490,000 species of plants. (That's 50 billion galaxies, 1×10^{12} stars, 48.5 million animal species, and 230,000 plant species more than mankind has classified or discovered.) I could have created all this in one hour. Actually, I could have created it in a second. But by taking my time, I wanted to demonstrate to the human race just how incredibly precious everything in creation is to me … including you.

PATENTS AND PUBLICATIONS:

1. Creation: Universal Patent no. 1
2. The Holy Bible

COMMUNITY ACTIVITIES:

On average I answer about four hundred thousand prayers every minute. Sometimes adults and children forget to pray, or don't know exactly how to pray or what to pray for. I understand. I also answer an extra eight million prayers a minute offered up on behalf of individuals by the Holy Spirit (see Rom. 8:26–27).

Moreover, I take great pleasure and interest in knowing every intimate detail of each person's life. I know every time you sit down, and every time you stand up. I even know the words in your mind before they reach your tongue (see Ps. 139:1–4). I know your secret desires, joys, hopes, and needs (see 1 Chron. 28:9), along with such details as the exact number of hairs on (or missing from) your head, the precise number of micrograms of plaque on your teeth, and the literal number of water molecules evaporating from your skin and lungs each second (see 1 John 3:20).

LANGUAGES SPOKEN: 6,000+

EXTRACURRICULAR ACTIVITIES:

Every day I take at least one supergiant star (1,000 times wider and 1 million times brighter than your galaxy's sun) and squeeze it together in my hands, setting off a spectacular supernova explosion. Then I take the core left behind, the neutron star (a teaspoon of it weighs more than a billion metric tons), and hold it between my fingertips. Standing directly over my "cosmic vacuum" (something you call a black hole), I release the star. No force in the universe—except me—can resist the gravitational pull of a black hole. Not even light! Instantly, the neutron star disappears—plunging into infinite density and creating a hyper nova with gamma ray bursts so strong that it outshines the rest of the universe! It's so incredibly beautiful! The intense burst of light and colors is utterly amazing! (In the beginning, I purposely stretched out the universe like a curtain [Isa. 42:5] making use of something you call "gravitational time dilation" to allow you the pleasure of seeing these spectacular explosions from earth today.)[1]

REFERENCES:

1. God the Son
2. God the Holy Spirit.

To say that this is an impressive résumé would be one of the biggest understatements in history. How would you react if this paper came across your desk? Would you not be completely blown away by just the knowledge that such a person even exists? What would happen if this individual were sitting directly across from you in a chair? What would you say? How would you act? Understandably, our minds become entangled in a sticky web of intangible realities trying to fathom such a far-out thought.

WHY DOESN'T GOD STOP EVIL?

Imagine instead that you're suddenly all alone in your office with the king or queen of England. What intelligent questions would you ask of your royal guest? Or what comments would you make? Would you make some remark about the weather? Or chitchat about the latest rookie signed by the New York Yankees? Would you not have tremendous difficulty even finding the proper words in the midst of your disordered thoughts?

What would happen if it weren't England's royalty sitting face-to-face with you—but heaven's royalty? How would you address so awesome a person as God? What questions would you ask someone who not only created every member of England's royal family but also tens of billions of black holes powerful enough to suck up light and entire stars?

The earth is 93 million miles away from the sun, and we can't even look at a solar eclipse without serious eye damage. From my childhood, I remember being herded into the darkened school gymnasium every time there was a solar eclipse so we wouldn't stare at the sun and suffer permanent damage to our little peepers. Imagine if God, whose glory is more luminous than every star in the universe, were sitting, not 93 million miles away, but *93 inches away in the same room.* Every atom in your body—and for millions of miles around—would be instantly vaporized into near nothingness! Even if God shielded you from the force of his overpowering glory, would you not find yourself totally dumbstruck, face planted into the carpet fibers, unable to breathe, unable to see, incapable of even whispering to God a plea that your life be spared?

Such a formidable visit actually occurred in the life of the apostle John, the writer of Revelation. Catching a glimpse of God's overpowering presence, whose countenance John described as "like the sun shining in all its brilliance," John fell forward instantly at God's feet as though dead (Rev. 1:16–17). Every time God allowed the brilliance of his being to be merely glimpsed by a man in the Scriptures, the man's mortal knees immediately gave way, and he fell face forward to the ground in a sort of worshipful daze—or dread.

That's why I'm more than just a little skeptical when some church leaders recount their casual encounters with God: "Here I was, driving down the highway, I glanced over, and there was God—sitting in the passenger seat!" Or, "There I was, cooking breakfast one morning, and God appeared out of nowhere to help me defrost the bacon." The laid-back conversations with God that usually follow are nothing short of ridiculous. If God had appeared to John while he was driving a car, the EMS crews would have needed an industrial crane to pry his body from the wreckage.

As King David declares, absolutely no one can fathom the greatness of our God (Ps. 145:3). David prayed these words before Israel's entire assembly: "Yours, O LORD, is the greatness and the power and the glory and the majesty and the splendor, for everything in heaven and earth is yours. Yours, O LORD, is the kingdom; you are exalted as head over all" (1 Chron. 29:11). Paul also described the majesty of God: "God, the blessed and only Ruler, the King of kings and Lord of lords, who alone is immortal and who lives in unapproachable light, whom no one has seen or can see. To him be honor and might forever. Amen" (1 Tim. 6:15–16).

Not only does God's greatness blow all the fuses in our imaginations but in the angels' imaginations as well. If every one of the trillions of stars in the universe, if every one of the trillions of living organisms on our planet—humans, animals, fungi, prokaryotes, and plants—if every object in the universe, living or nonliving, could cry out to God, each extolling a different aspect of God's supremacy, the universal chorus of praise would still fall pitifully short of capturing the dominion and infinite greatness of almighty God.

How great is our Lord! His power is absolute!
His understanding is beyond comprehension!

—PSALM 147:5 NLT

WHY DOESN'T GOD STOP EVIL?

God is King, robed and ruling, God is robed and surging with strength. And yes, the world is firm, immovable.

—PSALM 93:1 MSG

1
SCRUTINIZING THE RÉSUMÉ

Picture in your mind the following scenario:

One day you decide you want to demonstrate your love, so you go to the world's largest pet store and purchase six billion ants. Returning to your sprawling mansion, you toss all your cans of Raid into the dumpster and set loose the six billion tiny insects. "There you go, little ants. Enjoy your new home."

Suddenly, your life is consumed with looking after these minuscule creatures. You have five tons of dirt delivered to your home, then spend days shoveling it all through your house because ants like dirt—not carpet. You head off to work only long enough to buy the ants enough food, and then you race home to feed the hungry insects. You carefully monitor the room temperature and humidity to their liking. You park your car on the street so as not to disturb the tiny creatures on your garage floor. You sleep on the porch to allow the insects use of your bed (because they seem to really enjoy your Sealy Posturpedic mattress). And if the carpenter ants decide to make fine shavings out of the exquisite oak furniture that you personally handcrafted, that would be perfectly okay because that would be fulfilling their passions. And if the nasty fire ants decide to get under your clothes to bite you in some rather private areas, that's okay too because that's what some ants like to do. To even think about removing just one of these insects from your beautiful home would be totally out of the question.

Now you might be chuckling at the sheer absurdity (and stupidity) of such a scenario, but this isn't too far off from how most of the world views God: as some sort of cosmic caretaker whose sole function is to make sure that we, the more than six billion ants, are all having a grand old time here on one of his greatest creations we call Earth. "Just keep the good times rollin', God." And when the good times stop rollin', some come to the conclusion that this "cosmic caretaker" is merely a figment of our hyperactive imaginations. One boy, about to celebrate his bar mitzvah, said this to a team of interviewers for a *Life* magazine feature article: "God doesn't exist. If there was a god, and he was nice to me, he would let me get things I want, like a dog and cat, and to not be allergic."[1]

But I fear that I've committed a grave error in the analogy above. I hope I haven't led you to believe that the distance that exists between the majesty of God's being and us is similar to the distance that exists between us and ants. Actually, in relation to God's infinite and majestic being, we are far, far less than tiny insects. In fact, we are far less in comparison than the unicellular bacteria that inhabit the crevices and hairs of our bodies.

The importance of God's grandeur is grossly misunderstood by the world at large. We the clay (see Jer. 18:6) sometimes condemn God the Potter for seeking his own glory, making the Creator out to be some sort of conceited, selfish, egotistical superhero.

In a sense, God has no choice but to place his worth above every other living creature.

John Piper explains that for God to take delight in someone, or something, more than himself, would be idolatry. God "does all that he does to magnify the worth of his glory," asserts Piper. "He would be unrighteous if he valued anything more than what is supremely valuable, namely, himself."[2]

Not too long ago I heard a song with the lyrics, "You are the Father's obsession," referring to God's "obsession" for us. Well, God certainly does love us, but the central reference point of all his attention must first be himself. Celine Dion's words are closer to the truth: "That's the way it is." That's just the way it is with God. He is, in and of himself, self-contained, the definition of love, regardless of anyone else. How can someone as great as God our creator be "obsessed" with our imperfect beings? If the critics truly understood the greatness of God's majesty and just how much God has done for us, they'd understand that living for the glory of God is the only path in life that makes sense. They would also understand why God *cannot* place our worth above his worth.

According to Piper, the King of king's number one priority is this: "*The Chief end of God is to glorify God and enjoy himself forever.*"[3] Therefore, no matter how much evil there is in the world, God can never be downcast or discouraged. God can never be envious of the Donald Trumps and John Travoltas of this world because he is perpetually and infinitely happy in himself. We read in Psalm 115:3, "Our God is in heaven; he does whatever pleases him." Daniel proclaims that God, "does as he pleases with the powers of heaven and the peoples of the earth" (Dan. 4:35). Job writes, "But [God] stands alone, and who can oppose him? He does whatever he pleases" (Job 23:13). If God were exceedingly wise and powerful, why would he not work out events for his endless pleasure? Wouldn't you if you were God?

WHY DOESN'T GOD STOP EVIL?

All too often, though, we carry around this idea in the back of our minds that God exists only to satisfy *our* desires. "Hey, Potter!" shouts the arrogant piece of clay. "I'm not very happy with your decisions! *You owe me big time!*" If you can't get past the fact that God places *his* desires and *his* happiness above ours, you will never progress another step in this critical journey into understanding God more. The only "footprints" you will spy on this expedition will be your own. That is not to say that our heavenly Father isn't concerned with our happiness, or our desires. He definitely is. But if God were to place our earthly desires ahead of his desires, our worth above his majesty, our ignorance over his wisdom, and our imperfection above his holiness, he'd make a cosmic mockery of infinite magnitude of his altogether glorious being. It would be impossible for God to relinquish control of the universe to anyone—especially us.

The Potter does not exist for the clay's enjoyment. We exist solely for God's highest glory and endless pleasure (see Isa. 43:7). Parents owe their child love, protection, and guidance because they "borrowed" from the Creator the building blocks of life—unique blocks that came delivered to us with some strict moral rules. Because God created the entire universe out of nothing, only God holds the exclusive rights to everything we see, own, and use—including our own bodies. *We owe God absolutely everything. He owes us absolutely nothing.*

You might have been doing a double take these last few paragraphs. For how can God still be happy when his rebellious creatures commit billions of treacherous acts of sin—revolting spiritual adultery—day after day? If God works everything out to his good pleasure, how can he possibly look down upon all the death, suffering, and sin on this earth, and be just as happy as if he had never created us?

Piper shares with us more of his personal insight:

> How can God be happy and decree calamity? Consider that he has the capacity to view the world through two lenses. Through the narrow one he is grieved and angered at sin and pain. Through the wide one he sees evil in relation to its eternal purposes. Reality is like a mosaic. The parts may be ugly in themselves, but the whole is beautiful.[4]

SCRUTINIZING THE RÉSUMÉ

We look at the evil in our world and say, What was God thinking? Perhaps, though, we should be asking the question: What is God seeing from his perspective that we're not seeing from ours?

Life makes much more sense after scrutinizing God's résumé, and understanding a little more how almighty God views life through his "wide lens." We tend to view life through only the narrow lens and forget that God sees all the ugly pieces as a beautiful whole. The more we can view life from a top-down, divine perspective, the easier it will be to arrange our stepping-stones, and the more treasures we will uncover on our journey into answering the question *Why Doesn't God Stop Evil?*

AH, SOVEREIGN LORD!

The scientific facts known today are a stick of dynamite under the front porch of our spiritual complacency.[5]

"Spiritual complacency." Would such a pervasive evil of moral mediocrity, rebellious indifference, and gloomy reflection exist in the world if we truly understood the absolute sovereignty of almighty God? Would the existence of evil remain such a stumbling block to our faith if we were truly able to embrace the truth that God is in complete control of the world—including every aspect of our lives? "Ignorance of Providence is the greatest of all miseries," writes Calvin, "and the knowledge of it the highest happiness."[6]

To help us better understand the sovereignty of God, Charles Swindoll offers this simple definition:

> Sovereignty means our all-wise, all-knowing God reigns in realms beyond our comprehension to bring about a plan beyond our ability to alter, hinder, or stop.[7]

Remember I emphasized that *everything* God does is for his own good pleasure? The psalmist writes, "The LORD does whatever pleases him, in the heavens and on the earth, in the seas and all their depths"

WHY DOESN'T GOD STOP EVIL?

(Ps. 135:6). That pretty much covers every nook and cranny of creation, doesn't it? And *absolutely nothing* can rob God of one iota of his divine pleasure: no king, no judge, no celebrity, no terrorist, no virus, no nuclear warhead, no asteroid, no atheist, no international treaty, no NATO command force—not even the legions of demons and the Devil himself can frustrate God's purpose. *Nothing* will prevent God from accomplishing his perfect mosaic.

Swindoll goes on to explain:

> His plan includes all promotions and demotions. His plan can mean both adversity and prosperity, tragedy and calamity, ecstasy and joy. It envelops illness as much as health, perilous times as much as comfort, safety, prosperity, and ease…. It is at work through all disappointments, broken dreams, and lingering difficulties. And even when we cannot fully fathom why, He knows. Even when we cannot explain the reasons, He understands. And when we cannot see the end, He is there, nodding, "Yes, that is My plan."[8]

What I hope to tattoo across your heart here is the truth that our all-wise God utilizes a precise level of order to bring about his highest delight. No other achievable plan, or mosaic, could bring even a smidgen more delight and satisfaction to the heart of God—otherwise he'd "Just Do It," as the Nike slogan says. What happens today, God willed for his happiness an eternity ago.

> Remember the former things, those of long ago; I am God, and there is no other; I am God, and there is none like me. I make known the end from the beginning, from ancient times, what is still to come. I say: My purpose will stand, and I will do all that I please. (Isa. 46:9–10)

Perhaps you've never stopped to ponder God's desires, his purposes, and what he actually controls in the arena of life. If you're like many today who gaze on life from an "ant's perspective," you might be in for quite a shock in the rest of this book. Charles Spurgeon once said, "Men will allow God to be everywhere except on His throne."[9]

"While people reject the God of Scripture as their Sovereign," says the esteemed Bible teacher, Dr. John MacArthur, "they still claim Him as their servant. For some people that is *all* they mean by 'God Bless America.'"[10] God can be anywhere he wants to be as long as his goal is to prosper us, protect us, and make us happy; but as soon as he takes his rightful position on the throne as supreme ruler of the universe, we balk.

> The Lord has established his throne in heaven, and his kingdom rules over all. (Ps. 103:19)

Dr. MacArthur hits a sensitive nerve with this truth:

> We are so used to man-centered theology that if it doesn't start with us we can't understand it.... We are so proud, we are so self-centered, we are so man-centered in even our theology, that if it doesn't start with our choice we can't handle it.... We want to start with us and try to work our way back to God and hope He makes sense from our view.[11]

This is my favorite quotation in the book—and probably the entire book series—because it so effectively exposes one of the biggest problems in the church today that is causing most of the confusion over God's character. Read the quotation again carefully. Undoubtedly, the greatest hindrance to our understanding of God's sovereignty lies in our depraved state of self-centeredness and our ensuing "nursery school" view of God's dominion. We, the ants, want God, the Creator and Ruler of the universe, to foolishly put our wishes ahead of his perfections—our passions ahead of his flawless plans. We want God to sleep outside on the pavement and trek off to work each day, so that we can enjoy his beautiful home, the freshly delivered meals, and his comfy Sealy Posturpedic mattress. We are so human-centered in everything we do every second of every day, it is little wonder that the world is at a loss to understand God in the complicated matters of life. If we ever hope to understand God, we *must* start with the sovereign—not the servants. Stephen Charnock, a seventeenth-century Puritan, once said, "To slight his sovereignty, is to stab his deity."[12] We need to stop gazing on life with our self-centered, near-sighted, "narrow-lens" goggles, and start viewing life from a truly divine perspective.

To aid us in attaining this new perspective, we must perform one of the most humbling acts ever: We must look back on the fascinating mix of characters and the key events that have altered our destinies for the glory of God. These are the "footprints" of God in our lives. This is God's intricate handiwork shaping every second, every step, every thought we've ever had right from the moment of conception. Then, if you want to completely blow your mind, try taking a look back through history from a divine perspective to see God's footprints extending all the way back to the beginning of time. In doing so, you will gain a newfound appreciation and a raw excitement for the path-maker whom Paul extols as, "God, the blessed and only Ruler, the King of kings and Lord of lords" (1 Tim. 6:15b).

Let's start this humbling experience by first …

SCRUTINIZING GOD'S RÉSUMÉ

Most newly fired or laid-off employees dread the thought of having to put together yet another updated résumé. What do I list as my strengths? My weaknesses? Do I include my hobby of collecting hamster toenail clippings? Do I describe how fast I can stitch up the gaping abdominal hole in a warm corpse when I need to jump back on the helicopter ASAP to fly this guy's liver on ice in an Igloo cooler to an anxiously awaiting liver transplant team two hundred miles away? What will I write that will knock the socks off my next employer?

Picture, if you will, the monarch of England also sitting down one day to type up her personal résumé. "Hmmm," she thinks. "I wonder what I should write to convince my British subjects that I am fit to rule the country? I've never had to type out anything so … revealing."

Now that's pretty silly, isn't it? What king or queen of sound mind would commit such an absurd and humiliating act? He or she is already the sovereign.

SCRUTINIZING THE RÉSUMÉ

Imagine for a moment a world-renowned specialist of about fifty years of age, having had fourteen years of university training, having written more than a hundred research studies, and having traveled around the world to share his or her knowledge with the most brilliant minds on the globe, bending down on one knee to condense tens of thousands of hours of training and experience into thirty words in a soft voice to an eight-year-old. (It happens more often than you think.) Now picture this child pulling away with the disrespectful remark, "Yeah right. What do you know, Doc?"

No one would blame the medical doctor for just walking away. But instead, the specialist stays down on one knee and spends the next fifteen minutes kindly explaining to the naive child the rigorous training program required to be competent to treat this child's illness.

On a much greater scale, God has stooped to our diminutive level, like the kind, world-famous medical doctor stooping to the level of a child, to explain why he is competent to treat our "diseases" here on earth. God leaves his throne in heaven to descend to our level to kindly explain to us why he is more qualified than we to rule the universe. But we often just pull away with the attitude or action that asks, "What do you know, God?"

Who could blame God for walking away? Despite our heavenly Father's knowing that we would keep stabbing at his deity with our butcher knife of narcissistic pride, God, the King of kings, and Lord of lords, has, for some reason, "humbled" himself to the point where he has provided us with a copy of his "résumé" in the Holy Scriptures, kindly explaining to us why he alone is qualified to run this universe—along with our lives.

Interestingly, there are some who hold to something called "open theology." In a sense, God is seen by some as a ruler who is too perfect for his own liking. For life to be exciting for the Divine and fair for us mortals, God is said to voluntarily limit his powers so that he can't see around the next corner. These individuals believe that God is in the same old 1969 Dodge Charger RT—"the General Lee"—as the rest of us, racing through the Hazzard County of life at one hundred miles an hour with his hair on fire, taking random sideroads and jumping creeks like Bo and Luke Duke—not quite sure if there's going to be a boulder or a cow lying on the road around the next hairpin turn. And somehow, despite all the uncertainties and mishaps, God always manages to out-wit and out-maneuver "Boss Hogg"—the Devil.

Does this fit with God's résumé and his past (and future) work experience? Actually, it doesn't (see Job 40:1–2; Ps. 139:16; 1 John 3:20). For how can God claim perfect and sovereign reign over his cre-ation if he is ignorant of the affairs of his kingdom, incompetent to devise the best possible plan (because he doesn't know what's coming), and too weak and restricted to carry it out? Does God get himself into a sticky mess like Bo and Luke Duke, and then miraculously pull off a mind-blowing, high-flying stunt at the last second to save his hide?

I remember that in medical school one doctor flashed up an X-ray of a woman's chest and upper abdomen. We could hardly believe our eyes. The woman had swallowed more than two hundred metal objects! Safety pins, coins, nails, tacks—anything metal that she could get down her esophagus was sitting there in her stomach. I could just picture this deranged woman coming into the emergency room.

"Doc, I still don't feel so good."

"The blood tests we did this morning are all normal," replies the ER doctor. "What's the matter?"

"I've still got indigestion. My stomach feels kind of … full."

The doctor sighs. "Any vomiting, heartburn, chest pain, abdomi-nal pain, diarrhea, constipation, or blood in your stool?"

"No, just some minor indigestion."

"Well, like I said this morning, you probably just ate some bad chili down at the local fast-food restaurant last night. You'll be fine. Go home, take some Maalox, and don't call me in the morning. I'll be golfing."

Now, how would this doctor know that this woman had just swal-lowed more than two hundred metal objects if he didn't have the X-ray? (He'd soon find out when she started bleeding internally.) How could this doctor properly manage this patient without seeing the big picture? In the same way, I ask, how can God properly manage or rule this world without seeing the "big picture" of life? How can he describe himself as "the only wise God" (Rom. 16:27), with an understanding that "has no limit" (Ps. 147:5), if he can't see around the next corner? Could God claim to be all-knowing and all-powerful if he had to rely on us to tell him the results of the "X-rays"?

Therefore, to be the competent, sovereign ruler of the universe requires that one be a) all-knowing; b) all-wise; c) all-powerful; and d) absolutely free. If such a wise, all-knowing, and all-powerful God exists, don't you think he would want to communicate his truth to us by the most objective means possible? Wouldn't a doctor who has the power to heal want to communicate this to his or her patients? Why then is it so difficult to fathom that someone as intelligent as God would write down these answers for our spiritual sickness in black and white—in his one and only authorized autobiography?

Let's see if God fits the position of Sovereign Ruler of the universe by scrutinizing his résumé as written up for us in his number one best-selling book.

JOB QUALITIES FOR SOVEREIGN RULER:

All-Knowing

"His understanding has no limit," we read in Psalm 147:5b. God knows every time we sit down, lie down, stand up, or think. "You scrutinize my path and my lying down, and are intimately acquainted with all my ways. Even before there is a word on my tongue, behold, O LORD, you know it all" (Ps. 139:3–4 NASB). God "understands every motive behind the thoughts" (1 Chron. 28:9) and he knows (all-too-well) "the secrets of the heart" (Ps. 44:21). "Nothing in all creation is hidden from God's sight" (Heb. 4:13a). Not a sparrow falls without God knowing about it (see Matt. 10:29). And if we've missed anything, John says, "God is greater than our hearts, *and he knows everything*" (1 John 3:20b). He knows every single atom of your body so intimately that should you choose to have your remains cremated and scattered over a ten-mile stretch of ocean from an airplane, God will raise up every last atom on the final day and transform your natural body into a spiritual body (see 1 Cor. 15:42–44). That's how much God knows.

WHY DOESN'T GOD STOP EVIL?

All-Wise

Our Creator and Sovereign Lord is "the only wise God" (Rom. 16:27). "Oh, the depth of the riches of the wisdom and knowledge of God!" (Rom. 11:33a). "To God belong wisdom and power; counsel and understanding are his" (Job 12:13). So naturally, when we need wisdom, where should we turn? "If any of you lacks wisdom, he should ask God, who gives generously to all without finding fault, and it will be given to him" (James 1:5).

Just how wise is God? Well, according to one researcher, we make 300 to 17,000 decisions every day.[13] If you were to add up how many decisions you make between the ages of five and seventy-five, taking the lowest number of 300 per day, it would total almost 7.7 million decisions! Now, if it took you only four seconds to make the average decision, you have spent a minimum of 8,500 hours—or approximately one year of your life—scratching your brain, wondering what to do. If you are an indecisive individual, this is like four or five years.

Let's pretend you turned every single decision over to God. What would take you a year to do, God could accomplish in less than one second—and every decision would be absolutely perfect. Ever regretted a decision you've made? Maybe that boyfriend with the diabetic Chihuahua who you discovered three months into the relationship was already married to the mafia kingpin's daughter? Or that '92 car you bought that ended up on the front cover of, "*The World's Worst Lemons*"—five editions in a row? Consider this: Every day God makes more decisions in a second than you could make in a million lifetimes. And he hasn't regretted one decision yet.

That's how wise God is!

All-Powerful

> He brings princes to naught and reduces the rulers of this world to nothing. No sooner are they planted, no sooner are they sown, no sooner do they take root in the ground, than he blows on them and they wither, and a whirlwind sweeps

them away like chaff. "To whom will you compare me? Or who is my equal?" says the Holy One (Isa. 40:23–25).

Now to him who is able to do immeasurably more than all we ask or imagine, according to his power that is at work within us (Eph. 3:20).

Jesus looked at them and said, "With man this is impossible, but with God all things are possible" (Matt. 19:26).

"I am the Lord, the God of all mankind. Is anything too hard for me?" (Jer. 32:27)

Just how powerful is God? Let's say God wants to give you a front row seat to his biggest and most spectacular supernova explosion. Taking you in the palm of his hand, he gently sets you down on the edge of the biggest black hole in the universe. You look to your right. Then to your left. And suddenly all the rays of light for a hundred galaxies around are sucked past your eyes in the most dazzling, scintillating array of colors you've ever seen. All you can do is stare wide-eyed as God drops the neutron star into the black hole. Whoa. You thought the 2000 New Year's celebration at the Egyptian pyramids was stunning. This makes the millennium celebrations look like a toaster short circuiting. And through it all, the most powerful force in the universe is holding you from being pulled by the second most powerful force in the universe into utter blackness. Miraculously, your clothes, your hair, and your eyes are not ripped out of your body. Instead, the microscopic oil particles on your hair, the dirt under your fingernails, the plaque on your teeth, the lint and stains on your clothes, are instantly sucked into oblivion, leaving you the cleanest you've been since the good ol' days when mom scrubbed off half your epidermis in your Saturday night bath ritual.

And through it all, you haven't budged a millimeter.

That's how powerful God is!

Absolute Freedom

For the Lord Almighty has purposed, and who can thwart him? His hand is stretched out, and who can turn it back (Isa. 14:27)?

WHY DOESN'T GOD STOP EVIL?

> There is no wisdom, no insight, no plan that can succeed against the LORD (Prov. 21:30).
>
> But he stands alone, and who can oppose him? He does whatever he pleases. (Job 23:13)

How much liberty does God have? If you were placed in front of a firing squad composed of fifty of the world's top snipers aiming AK-47s at your body, God, at his discretion, could easily and freely accomplish any of the following:

1. Not allow one bullet to touch your body.
2. Redirect the path of each bullet, shave each one down with a specific razor edge, and give you a better haircut than you could receive at any salon in Beverly Hills.
3. Replace fifty of the top snipers in the world with fifty of the worst snipers in the world, and redirect every one of the stray bullets through the center of your forehead.

No matter how accurate or inaccurate a firing squad is, or what type of guns they are using, it makes no difference to God. He would have just as much freedom to spare your life or to end it right there on the spot.

Don't misunderstand me here; it's not that God is a capricious being, flitting through the world with a "drive-by shooting" mentality—not caring who lives and who dies. That's certainly not the God I wholeheartedly serve. But God alone created us, along with this entire universe. He owes nothing to anyone. He has no favors to repay. He has no boss, no high court, no government, and no Howard Sterns telling him what he should and shouldn't do. God is just as free to make a decision in his perfect character that spares a life as he is to take a life. He is so free, in fact, that he is not even bound by the constraints of time. Imagine living a life where you had as much time to do whatever you want, whenever you want, however you want, in any galaxy you want, with no care in the world about where you had to be Monday morning.

That's how much freedom God has.

SCRUTINIZING THE RÉSUMÉ

After closely studying these verses, it is obvious that God has all the necessary qualities—and more—for the job as supreme ruler. But to what extent does he exercise his right to rule? Perhaps he takes extended vacations on company time.

JOB PERFORMANCE STATS:

Ruler over Nature

God says, "I dry up the sea, I turn rivers into a desert" (Isa. 50:2b). "He causes his sun to rise on the evil and the good, and sends rain on the righteous and the unrighteous" (Matt. 5:45b). Lightning, thunder, snow, hurricanes, clouds, rain, atmospheric pressure changes, and the tilting of the earth on its axis do not occur except by God's will (see Job 37:3–13; Ps. 107:25; Dan. 2:21).

Moreover, the Almighty preserves the life of every beast on an ongoing basis (see Ps. 36:6), holding in his hand the life essence of every creature (see Job 12:10). He daily supplies food for the beasts of the field and the birds of the air (see Ps. 147:9). How can we help but agree with Elihu when he said, "God's voice thunders in marvelous ways; he does great things beyond our understanding" (Job 37:5)?

Consider this: There are hundreds of zoos, aquariums, wildlife parks, and animal sanctuaries scattered around the world, many requiring hundreds of workers to monitor and care for the animals and birds. The world famous San Diego Zoo and San Diego Wildlife Park together have more than 3,200 individual birds, and more than 1,300 species and subspecies. If you take the hundreds of thousands of birds and animals in all the zoos worldwide, the total still pales in comparison to the number of creatures roaming free on the planet. Who do you think is the zookeeper looking after them? God's zoo is bigger than all the zoos in the world combined—and he runs it himself.

Best of all, there's no admission fee.

WHY DOESN'T GOD STOP EVIL?

Ruler over Mankind

God determined in eternity exactly the moment in history when you and I would be born, where we would live (see Acts 17:26), and when we would die (see Job 14:5). God provides the very oxygen molecules we breathe each minute (see Job 12:10). He supplies our food and water (see Ps. 107:9). And he is directly responsible for the salvation of souls (see Eph. 1:4; 2 Thess. 2:13). He is ultimately responsible for guiding the very steps of men and women (see Prov. 20:24) and dishing out to each individual all the wisdom, understanding, and knowledge he or she will ever attain (see Dan. 2:21). "The Lord sends poverty and wealth; he humbles and he exalts" (1 Sam. 2:7). God even controls who gets what from lottery winnings—right down to the last penny (see Prov. 16:33).

"He makes nations great, and destroys them; he enlarges nations, and disperses them" (Job 12:23). God has raised to power and leadership every king, president, dictator, CIA officer, and policeman who has ever lived or will ever live (see Rom. 13:1). The King of Glory directs the hearts of earthly kings like you and I would direct a trickle of water by taking a stick and plowing a path from a mud puddle (see Prov. 21:1). God protects nations (see Isa. 41:10–11), and he frustrates them (see Ps. 33:10).

Did you know that more than one hundred thousand employees work at the Walt Disney Company and its affiliates throughout the world in more than twenty-seven hundred job classifications? This doesn't even include the thousands they have to hire at theme parks and resorts during peak summer hours. Some people have never been to a Disney park or resort to see Mickey and Minnie; others have shaken hands with the famous pair dozens of times. It takes tens of thousands of people to entertain only a fraction of the world's population for the odd day trip. What would happen if all the people in the world—six and a half billion and counting—decided to show up at the Disney theme parks and resorts on the same day? How many employees would it take to look after all these customers for just twelve hours?

Well, God manages the fine details of the lives of more than six billion people every minute of every day. And he does it himself—without pay and vacation time—and without making one mistake.

SCRUTINIZING THE RÉSUMÉ

Imagine if you could find someone like that to run your business.

Administrator of Good and Evil

Joseph said to his brothers,

> You intended to harm me, but God intended it for good to accomplish what is now being done, the saving of many lives. (Gen. 50:20)

God, in his eternal purpose, decided beforehand that Herod and Pontus Pilate would be the ones to bring about the crucifixion of Christ (see Acts 4:27–28).

> The Lord said to him, "Who gave man his mouth? Who makes him deaf or mute? Who gives him sight or makes him blind? Is it not I, the Lord?" (Ex. 4:11).
>
> I form the light and create darkness, I bring prosperity and create disaster; I, the Lord, do all these things (Isa. 45:7).
>
> The Lord works out everything for his own ends—even the wicked for a day of disaster. (Prov. 16:4)

In the United States in 2004, there were approximately 2.1 million prisoners in federal or state prisons or in local jails. Every now and again we hear of someone who has been wrongly imprisoned, like Joseph was in Bible times. Every prisoner in America's prison system, and in every prison system around the world, whether guilty or innocent, is there under God's control. Yes, God sometimes even allows innocent people to be put behind bars.

Now, some of these prisoners have criminal records the size of a small novel. Every act of evil committed by every criminal in the world has served some purpose in God's sovereign plan. God is the administrator of good—and he is the administrator of evil. It is no harder for God to work the millions of murders, thefts, assaults, and drunk driving charges into his sovereign game plan for his glory, than it is to fit together all the good deeds done since the beginning of time.

The saint and the criminal are both useful to God's purposes.

WHY DOESN'T GOD STOP EVIL?

If our all-wise Creator controls and sustains all the elements and laws of nature to such a mind-boggling order of precision; if our all-powerful Creator upholds the life of every living creature on the face of the earth by daily providing indispensable oxygen, food, and water; if our all-knowing God is currently directing the hearts of kings and leaders for his own wise purposes; if mankind's every step, every thought, and every word, whether good or evil, is being governed and used by our sovereign God at this very moment for his greatest glory, is there *anything* that God doesn't have complete control over?

Our times are *definitely* in God's hands (Ps. 31:15).

Those who argue that God rarely interacts in the affairs of his creation haven't read his official autobiography. Those who believe that our universe has somehow spun wildly out of his control or think that God wound up the universe like a clock and walked away are often the ones who would rather use a *Cliff's Notes* version of God's autobiography—rather than just read it.

> For everything comes from him; everything exists by his power and is intended for his glory. To him be glory evermore. Amen. (Rom. 11:36 NLT)

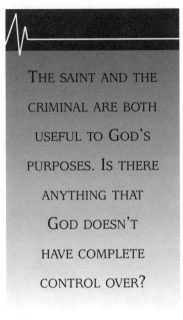

THE SAINT AND THE
CRIMINAL ARE BOTH
USEFUL TO GOD'S
PURPOSES. IS THERE
ANYTHING THAT
GOD DOESN'T
HAVE COMPLETE
CONTROL OVER?

WHY DOESN'T GOD STOP EVIL?

When a trumpet sounds in a city, do not the people tremble? When disaster comes to a city, has not the LORD caused it?

—AMOS 3:6

2
WHAT ABOUT MY MANGOS?

To the horror of many of you, I have ripped open a giant vat of worms in the last chapter and seemingly tossed the lid into a bottomless ravine. "You mean to say that God governs absolutely *everything* in life—including all sickness, death, wars, famine, earthquakes, and tsunamis? Are you telling me that God was in complete control when thousands of mothers and fathers in the tsunami disaster in December 2004 watched in terror as one or all of their children were swept out into the ocean—never to be seen again? A mother who carried her precious baby for nine months in her womb watched, utterly helpless, as the waves ripped her son from her grasp. His screams will resonate in her ears till the day she dies. How can this possibly be consistent with the character of the all-loving, all-wise, all-knowing, and all-powerful divine being taught in Sunday school every week around the globe?"

Certainly these questions do not come with neatly wrapped answers to pacify everyone's anger or satisfy our curiosity. But if God is in complete control of every aspect of the universe, as the multitude of Scripture verses we've looked at so clearly demonstrate, then we must believe that absolutely *nothing* happens outside of God's divine jurisdiction without his approval. No kidnapping, murder, suicide, war, or natural disaster can take place apart from either God's permissive will (that is, what he permits) or directive will (the direct actions he himself performs). Regardless, we should "give thanks in all circumstances," as Paul writes to believers, "for this is God's will for you in Christ Jesus" (1 Thess. 5:18).

Hank Hanegraaff passionately remarks:

> If you take one molecule away from the sovereignty of God you don't have theism—you have atheism. If God isn't Sovereign over everything, He isn't God.[1]

With verses so crystal clear on the absolute sovereignty of God, you might think that the Ruler of heaven and earth can somehow be charged with the crime of evil if he permits it. But I ask, if you eat a nutritious mushroom for the nourishment of your body one day, and the next, eat a poisonous mushroom and die an ugly death within five days, is the sun to blame for shining upon the good mushroom as well as the bad mushroom, causing both to grow? Can you blame the sun if you ingest one of fifty species of poisonous mushrooms that fries your liver because you were convinced by all the advertising hype that "all natural" products are always healthy for you? What each plant does with the sun's sustaining rays does not incriminate the sun. Or imagine a surgeon who is being sued for negligence standing up in court and saying, "I'm not responsible for amputating the wrong leg. God is to blame because he created me and gave me the strength to cut it off." What we decide to do with God's sustaining power does not incriminate God.[2] God cannot be charged with negligence, or the crime of evil, even though he foresees and permits it for his own good use (see Rom. 9:19–20; James 1:13).

Now, you might counter, "Yes, but if God can foresee evil, is he not morally responsible for what happens to us? If he knew the surgeon would cut off the healthy leg by mistake, wouldn't God be guilty if he didn't try to stop him? Or if I knew that a robber were going to go to your house tonight, tie you up, and shoot you dead, would I not be guilty for not warning you?"

Yes, *I* would be morally guilty in part if I didn't warn you, because God has commanded us to respect and value human life—and to love our neighbor.[3] We are under obligation to God and his creation because he created everything. But to whom is God under obligation, argues Charnock, "since the infinite transcendency of his nature and his sovereign dominion frees him from any such obligation?"[4] If a farmer is not obligated to a chicken to preserve the bird's life, or to a cornstalk to keep it standing—neither of which he actually created—how can God be obligated in any way to us, whom he did create?

Where do we get the warped idea that the Potter actually owes the clay something—especially when we've mutinied against our Maker and done utterly nothing to merit God's love and mercy? Where do we get off criticizing and arguing with our infinite God who knows the end from the beginning and every detail in between?

> Destruction is certain for those who argue with their Creator. Does a clay pot ever argue with its maker? Does the clay dispute with the one who shapes it, saying, "Stop, you are doing it wrong!" Does the pot exclaim, "How clumsy can you be!" (Isa. 45:9 NLT)

This is the story of a kind-hearted general internist in his forties who became disillusioned one day with his managed-care medical practice. For years he had been unfairly criticized by patients and his peers for scheduling too many patients in his clinics. The truth is, he felt guilty for turning away any who genuinely needed his help. Unfortunately, the end result was overbooked clinics and unfair criticisms that he was miserly with his time.

One day he shocked everyone by hanging a "closed" sign on his medical clinic doors. He sold his convertible Mercedes and his half-million-dollar home. And with the money, he bought a plane ticket to Nigeria and enough drugs to treat dozens of AIDS patients for several months.

News spread throughout a tiny Nigerian village that the "white miracle doctor" had arrived to treat the dying. Hundreds of sick men, women, and children, many infected with HIV ran, hobbled, or were carried on stretchers to a small mud hut on the outskirts of the village. There, the doctor examined each person, dispensing enough medications to keep each person alive for at least another year. Most were so thankful for the doctor's care, they brought what little they had—carvings and baskets of fruit—and laid them at the doctor's feet.

One day the doctor reached into his medical bag. Moving his hand around inside, he frowned. Suddenly, he heard cursing and shouting coming from outside his door. The village witch doctor, somewhat sickly looking and angrier than a televangelist at a SpongeBob SquarePants convention, barged past everyone to the front of the line, menacingly waving a jagged knife.

"If you don't leave, I will kill you," he hissed—his voice a little hoarse.

"If I don't leave," the medical doctor replied in a calm voice, "you will soon be out of business. Fortunately for you, I have only enough medication to treat five more patients."

"And then you will leave."

"I probably will."

"Or I'll kill you!"

The witch doctor grunted his disgust, then rushed toward the door—his bare back exposing tiny skin lesions to the medical doctor.

"You're dying, aren't you?"

The witch doctor spun around.

The doctor continued. "Those lesions on your back are Kaposi's Sarcoma. Cancer. A manifestation of AIDS."

"You are a demon!" shouted the witch doctor.

"I am a medical doctor with medication that can spare your life."

"I don't need your fat seeds."

WHAT ABOUT MY MANGOS?

"Without my medication you will die, and I will have no competition in this village."

The witch doctor's tongue went limp. The doctor picked up his bag, turned it upside down, and emptied all the medication he had left on the rickety wooden table.

"There's enough medication here to keep you alive for five years. It's all yours ... if you want it."

The witch doctor hesitated for a moment ... then snatched up the medication in his hands. He put the knife to the doctor's throat. "If you ever tell anyone, I'll—"

"Kill you," finished the MD, his eyes wide. "I know."

Two days later, as the doctor was packing up to leave the village, a young man, coughing violently, hobbled into his hut. The doctor immediately recognized him as the next AIDS patient in the line that hadn't received medication.

"The witch doctor is still telling everyone in the village that you are possessed by an evil spirit."

"I know."

"He has put more voodoo curses on you than anyone else."

"I know."

"You gave—" The young male coughed and coughed, unable to catch his breath. "You gave five times more magic seeds to the witch doctor than anyone else. Why did you do that? It's not fair."

The medical doctor dropped his stethoscope into his doctor's bag and moved slowly past the man. Reaching the hut's door, he turned around.

"Who paid for the magic pills?" asked the MD.

"White miracle doctor."

"Who brought the magic pills from America?"

"White miracle doctor."

"Who deserves the magic pills?"

"Me."

"What did you give me for the pills?"

"Two mangos."

"Those mangos may have been all you possessed," said the MD,

WHY DOESN'T GOD STOP EVIL?

"but they could never come close to paying for a year's worth of medication to treat your AIDS."

The young Nigerian shamefully dropped his head.

The doctor gently continued, "Because the magic white seeds are mine, I can give them to anyone I want, in any amount I want. No one deserved a single pill, so I am completely fair."

"But why did you give them to the witch doctor who hates you? Why not me?"

The medical doctor placed his hand on the man's shoulder. "Everyone in the village knew he was dying. That witch doctor, alive and well, will do more in five years of cursing my name to proclaim my generosity and grace, than a hundred villagers praising my name for decades to come."

The medical doctor extended a friendly hand to the man, but the Nigerian again dropped his head—unwilling to bring his hand up. The doctor slowly lowered his outstretched hand, nodded good-bye, then turned, strolling out of the hut to meet the entire village, which had gathered to bid good-bye to the bighearted "white miracle doctor" who brought hope and life to their small Nigerian village.

This story really hits home in my heart. Often, we are like this young AIDS patient, coming to God with our two mangos, wondering why, instead of giving his life-saving magic seeds to us to keep us alive and healthy and prosperous for just one more year, he has given his magic seeds to someone else. With our two hands, we point to our two feet, then to our two ears, our two lips, and our two eyes, and say, "God, look what I've given to you. I—not that person—*deserve* your magic seeds. Do I not deserve to live in health and happiness?"

But God gently puts his hand on our shoulder, and replies, "My dear child. Your two mangos can never come close to repaying even the life-sustaining oxygen molecules I give you each and every day. Not one living organism in all of my creation deserves one thing from me. That is why when I give my 'magic seeds' to those who hate me the most, they will do more in five years of cursing my name to proclaim my generosity and grace, than a hundred saints praising my name for decades to come."

WHAT ABOUT MY MANGOS?

After God had permitted Satan to bring down a desert wind, killing all of Job's sons and daughters, Job implored his friends, "If he sends death to snatch someone away, who can stop him? Who dares to ask him, 'What are you doing?'" (Job 9:12 NLT). Remember the important point made earlier: We owe our Creator *absolutely everything*. He owes us *absolutely nothing*. (No matter how many "mangos" we give him.) This is something that I estimate less than one percent of the world's population truly understands.

May we keep this in the back of our minds throughout this book series: The only thing our loving heavenly Father will ever hand us that we don't deserve is his unparalleled grace. That grace—God's "magic seeds"—is comprised of everything he gives us that we don't deserve: the oxygen we breathe; the children we conceive; health and prosperity of any kind—even the strength to take a deep breath, exhale, adduct our vocal cords, and twist our tongue in odd positions to sing praises to his name. All of this we don't deserve. Sending his son, Jesus Christ, to Earth to die for our sins was God's greatest display of grace and goodness. Therefore, God's grace is something infinitely more valuable than money; it is something we can take to our soul's bank and deposit for all of eternity.

WHY DOESN'T GOD STOP EVIL?

All sin in its nature is contempt
of the divine dominion.[1]

—STEPHEN CHARNOCK

3

QUESTIONING THE WHIRLWIND

Given that God is the only person qualified to run this universe, when evil erupts, our minds naturally gravitate to questions surrounding the Almighty's competency. Many people think that God should list the existence of evil as one of his weaknesses on his divine résumé.

The term *evil* has been applied to almost everything in our day, including nuclear weapons, terrorists, hurricanes, viruses, sickness, and hideous haircuts. We toss around the term so much that many of us would be hard-pressed to come up with a decent definition of evil other than, "It's something really, really bad." Furthermore, *evil* seems to be perspective dependent. For instance, in the Western world, Bin Laden, Al-Qaeda, and all other terrorists are considered evil, while the American president is considered good. (By most Americans, that is.) But in parts of the East, the terrorists are considered good, and every American president evil.

Instead of asking, "What do I think is evil?" maybe the real question we should ask is, "What does *God* define as evil?" Isn't this the question that really matters? Let's say we attach some helpful definitions to the term *evil* and explore the consequences of such in an attempt to better understand why God allows evil, and to see more precisely how God goes about limiting the amount of wickedness in our world.

To accomplish this, let's journey back to the beginning of time and work ourselves forward. In doing so, we'll come to better understand how God's "law of sin" (Rom. 5:12–21; 8:2) is an integral part of our everyday lives.[2]

DISSECTING THE WHIRLWIND

> They sow the wind and reap the whirlwind. (Hos. 8:7a)

We are obligated to warn our fellow neighbor of an impending tragedy such as a violent house invasion or a raging wildfire. God, on the other hand, is under no such obligation because, as our Creator, he does not owe us anything. Nevertheless, God *has* actually warned us beforehand about the consequences of sin and evil (see Rom. 6:23). In Genesis 2:17, God warned Adam and Eve, "But you must not eat from the tree of the knowledge of good and evil, for when you eat of it you will surely die." The Hebrew here is literally, "dying thou shalt die"—dying spiritually, they would also one day die physically.

What exactly happened to Adam and Eve's DNA the specific instant they ate the forbidden fruit we don't know. Scientists have proposed many theories for why we all age and die, most of which center around the defects in our deoxyribonucleic acid (DNA). Some experts on the subject of aging believe that our DNA has been damaged by the loss of specialized DNA sequences known as telomeres that function to maintain chromosomal length.[3] Whatever happened in the garden of Eden, both spiritual and physical death have been passed down (spread throughout) every succeeding generation (see Rom. 5:12). We are consequently born "unclean" with sin-cracked natures that make our inner cores appear ugly to God and keep us separated from his holy being (see Eph. 2:3).

Jesus tried to explain this to his disciples:

QUESTIONING THE WHIRLWIND

> What comes out of a man is what makes him "unclean." For from within, out of men's hearts, come evil thoughts, sexual immorality, theft, murder, adultery, greed, malice, deceit, lewdness, envy, slander, arrogance and folly. All these evils come from inside and make a man "unclean." (Mark 7:20–23)

The evil Jesus is speaking of here can be defined as an act, belief, or nature contrary in some way to God. (Refer to the diagram below, "Consequences of Evil.") This evil includes not only our actions, but also the very core of our beings. It's not like the dirt particles that collect on our hands that we can just wash off and be done with. Even Paul the superapostle wrote, "Evil is present in me" (Rom. 7:21 NASB). We're stuck with our "cracked natures," our evil core, right from the moment of conception (Ps. 51:5).

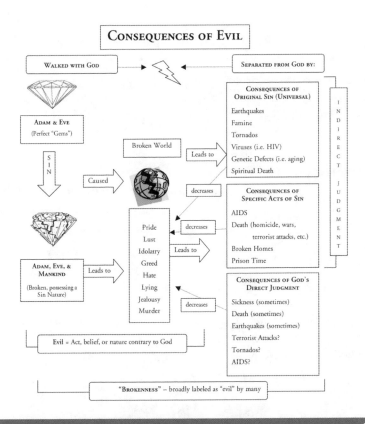

CONSEQUENCES OF EVIL

WALKED WITH GOD → ⚡ ← SEPARATED FROM GOD BY:

ADAM & EVE (Perfect "Gems")

SIN

ADAM, EVE, & MANKIND (Broken, possessing a Sin Nature)

Leads to

Broken World — Leads to

Caused → 🌍

Pride
Lust
Idolatry
Greed
Hate
Lying
Jealousy
Murder

Leads to

decreases
decreases
decreases

CONSEQUENCES OF ORIGINAL SIN (UNIVERSAL)
Earthquakes
Famine
Tornados
Viruses (i.e. HIV)
Genetic Defects (i.e. aging)
Spiritual Death

CONSEQUENCES OF SPECIFIC ACTS OF SIN
AIDS
Death (homicide, wars, terrorist attacks, etc.)
Broken Homes
Prison Time

CONSEQUENCES OF GOD'S DIRECT JUDGMENT
Sickness (sometimes)
Death (sometimes)
Earthquakes (sometimes)
Terrorist Attacks?
Tornados?
AIDS?

INDIRECT JUDGMENT

Evil = Act, belief, or nature contrary to God

"BROKENNESS" – broadly labeled as "evil" by many

WHY DOESN'T GOD STOP EVIL?

Though different from Jesus' definition, most citizens on our planet consider evil to be some misfortune or calamity, such as tornadoes, famine, earthquakes, or even genetic defects. Anything that brings sorrow and distress is often labeled "evil." But let's say we ascribe to all these things the term *brokenness*.

Regardless of whom we wish to blame for the evil all around us, all of this brokenness is ultimately the result of mankind's original sin. When Adam and Eve sinned in the garden, God, in his righteous judgment, pronounced certain curses upon nature, mankind, and Satan. (These curses were just as rational from God's viewpoint as the jail time we would consider rational for murder.) What many people label "evil" or a "misfortune"—such as famines, tornadoes, cancer, earthquakes, and physical death—are actually the result of God's *indirect judgment* in the curses he pronounced in the garden of Eden.[4] Because God *always* executes his judgment on sin in strict accordance with his holiness and moral law, it is *always* fair and sensible. When God pronounces a curse, the punishment always fits the crime perfectly. Naturally, the world can't understand this because we are the ones who have fallen under the curse. Humanity "drinks up evil like water!" we read in Job 15:16. Rarely will the perpetrator of a crime agree with the punishment handed out.

When God judged the entire human race, one curse included physical death from any cause—be it accidental (e.g., car crashes), deliberate (e.g., murder), or natural (e.g., aging) (see Gen. 3:19). Included, I believe, in this curse was a "sub-curse" that involved pain and suffering. God told Eve that her pains in childbearing would "greatly increase" (v. 16).

Now what exactly had changed in Eve's body that would now make childbirth a very painful process? Did God curse the female gender by suddenly shrinking Eve's pelvis, making the birth canal only half as large? Did Eve originally have hips that were twice as wide as her shoulders? (Talk about being "big-boned"!) Or did God originally intend for babies to be born at only a fraction of the size they are today? Why would Eve now have increased pain in childbearing?

QUESTIONING THE WHIRLWIND

What Was God thinking?

The Bible doesn't say specifically, but I believe this curse also extended to men. No, I'm not saying God intended for men to have babies; I am saying that perhaps God originally created Adam and Eve with a perfectly functioning natural pain-killing system that would easily handle persistent and extreme amounts of pain—such as the pain involved in giving birth to an eight- or ten-pound baby, or breaking a leg. Because God told Eve her pains in childbirth would "greatly increase," that may provide us a clue that God originally created the human body in a perfect world to have some measure of discomfort during the birthing process. After studying the human nervous system, it would appear that an obnoxious sensation of some sort is beneficial because it warns an individual, for example, that a baby is coming or that his or her hand is frying on the stovetop (a keen sense of smell would help too). For instance, leprosy patients (Hansen's disease) lose their distal appendages because they first lose feeling in their hands, feet, and face, and often injure themselves unknowingly.

But extreme, unbearable pain in a perfect, disease-free body is of no value whatsoever. So when Adam and Eve sinned, their natural pain killing system responsible for sending out massive amounts of endorphins (the body's natural pain killers) was probably damaged—including the genetic coding for such. A similar gene-damaging event probably started the aging process. This curse meant that the human race would now experience intense pain, not only in childbirth but also in trauma (e.g., broken bones) and disease (cancer). Adam and Eve's original sin somehow "fractured" our DNA, bringing about death and the potential for severe pain; but it also, in some way, "fractured" the rest of our natural creation (Rom. 8:22).

God also cursed the ground (see Gen. 3:17–19), allowing for the existence of thorns and weeds. It's possible that God's curses at this stage opened up the world to such natural disasters as tornadoes, hurricanes, earthquakes, volcanic eruptions, and deadly plagues including harmful microorganisms such as tuberculosis bacterium and HIV.

WHY DOESN'T GOD STOP EVIL?

God also cursed Satan at that moment, sentencing him to a crushing defeat one day at the hands of his Son, Jesus Christ (vv. 14–15).

Who then is ultimately responsible for all these "evils" besieging us? It was because of humankind's sin that God cursed the world in the first place. Therefore, it isn't God, *but humans* who are ultimately responsible for the "brokenness" we see all around us: sickness, extreme pain, viruses, plagues, earthquakes, tsunamis, physical and spiritual death. Because Adam and Eve sowed "the wind," we all reaped "the whirlwind" (see Hos. 8:7). But God's judgment—the "whirlwind"—didn't drop upon the human race as the result of a momentary lapse of saneness brought about by a fit of divine anger. No, God's judgment was carefully meted out in accordance with his perfect justice and holiness to wisely accomplish some very specific objectives.

God's justice, an "eye for eye, and tooth for tooth" (Ex. 21:24; cf. Matt. 5:38), is termed "retaliatory" because the punishment for a perpetrator's crime is both directly and fairly connected to the rebellious act. When Adam and Eve brought about pain to the heavenly Father's heart, God brought pain to the human race. When the pair broke the core of his moral law, God likely broke their core—their DNA. "Adam and Eve sinned by eating; they would suffer in order to eat.... The serpent destroyed the human race; he will be destroyed."[5]

But this tragic story has a happy ending. As horrendous as these consequences of evil are, our loving heavenly Father provided a means whereby mankind could be redeemed from the snares of evil. When God cursed the serpent Satan, telling him that the woman's offspring "will crush your head" (Gen. 3:15). God was already looking ahead on his "personal time line" to that great day when Christ will strike the final blow and finish "crushing" the head of Satan, allowing Christ to rule over all the earth with us as his bride (see Rev. 12:17; 20:1–3, 10).

In reality, God dropped the biggest "plot twist" in the history of "plot twists" when he sent his Son, Jesus Christ, to earth to die on the cross and redeem us from our sins. (As seen above, he did give us clues in the first half of his autobiography to let us know that something really big in history was about to happen.) God said, "I don't care that these people possess only two mangos each (mangos that I, incidentally, gave them), I'm going to give them enough of my grace—my "magic seeds"—to keep them alive for eternity with me. I created hell and I can, sure as hell exists, create a way to keep people out of hell—because I also created happy endings. No more an eye for an eye. Now it's two eyes. Two ears. Two hands. Two feet. Two lungs. Two immaterial parts of your body—your heart and your soul. Both "mangos." I expect everything that a person will take into eternity in exchange for everything I have to offer for all of eternity. Doesn't this seem fair? Saving faith, repentance, and submission of one's life to me in exchange for my life-saving "magic seeds" of grace will provide life for not just one year or five years, but for all of eternity.

> For God so loved the world that he gave his one and only
> Son, that whoever believes in him shall not perish but have
> eternal life. (John 3:16)

PUTTING THE WHIRLWIND INTO PERSPECTIVE

Studying the diagram "Consequences of Evil," you'll notice that I've categorized these consequences as being caused by

1. original sin (Adam and Eve's sin in the garden)
2. specific acts of sin
3. God's direct judgment

You'll also notice that the consequences of evil, such as wars, aging, earthquakes, and broken homes, listed under "original sin" and "specific acts of sin," are labeled as God's "indirect judgment."

When we develop cancer, lose our home in a tornado, or die in a car accident, this is essentially God's *indirect* judgment stemming back to man's original sin in the garden of Eden. This isn't instant divine retaliation for a specific sin. This is not God saying, "Joe cheated on his wife, so now I'm going to strike him down with prostate cancer. Then I'm going to reduce his house to splinters in a tornado. Then, just to be sure he gets everything that's coming to him, I'm going to put him on a collision course with an eighteen wheeler hauling cement culverts!" This is not how our God works. Tragedy and death are simply our earned wages from our sinful nature inherited from Adam and Eve (see Rom. 6:23). Our defective genes and our "cracked" world came via Adam and Eve's choice to deliberately disobey God.

In addition to God's indirect judgment, there definitely are instances throughout Scripture in which God poured out his direct judgment—his holy wrath and holy lightning bolts—with his "bare hands," as we might say. God wiped out mankind, save Noah and his family, with a flood (see Gen. 8). God utterly destroyed Sodom and Gomorrah with fire and brimstone (see Gen. 19:24). God struck Zechariah with dumbness for a time (see Luke 1:20). And God killed Ananias and his wife Sapphira on the spot for telling a lie (see Acts 5:1–10). Some believers point to these events to say that *all* tornadoes, *all* earthquakes, *all* floods, and *all* sickness are the *direct* judgment of God for an individual or nation's wickedness.

You'll notice that I've placed question marks beside some consequences of evil under the heading, "God's Direct Judgment." I don't presume to know the mind of God, but I'm surprised by how many people do. Take for instance those who passionately declare that God is directly judging the homosexual community right now with AIDS. How is it that *they* know the mind of God so precisely? I'll admit I have an opinion: I personally believe that AIDS, which now affects almost equal numbers of homosexuals and heterosexuals around the world, is God's *indirect* judgment on humanity in general—little difference from God using the SARS virus in his indirect judgment.[6] But how can any of us know for sure? Remember, God is sovereign; he does not exist to back up what we believe.

By neglecting to see the difference between God's direct and indirect judgment, many people, believers and unbelievers alike, become wracked with guilt because they think that sickness is God's way of directly punishing them, or their loved ones, for some specific act of sin they committed. If my child is born with a cleft lip, this is God's way of punishing me for all the drugs I did back in college. If I develop diabetes, this is God's way of getting back at me for all my affairs. Or if I'm maimed in a car crash, this is God's way of getting back at me for my wild years of promiscuous sex and alcoholism as a teenager. Sickness is frequently equated with God's fiery lightning bolts of judgment.

Hopefully, what I say next will clear up this pervasive misunderstanding. Though Scripture does teach that an individual's sickness is sometimes directly linked to his or her sin (see Acts 12:23; 1 Cor. 11:30), such lightning bolts of divine justice, in our day at least, are uncommon. I know that some evangelicals would strongly disagree with me on this point, but after years of medical study I honestly can't see a significant connection. Yes, party-till-you-drop lifestyles are intricately linked to sickness. If you smoke for decades, you have a much higher risk of developing lung, throat, and bladder cancer; if you have sex with several partners, your chances of contracting HIV, herpes, or cervical cancer (if you're a woman) are significantly increased. But these are just the natural consequences of foolish and sinful actions. It is not God's way of setting aside his "tools" to reach down with his bare hands to physically place a cancer cell in one of your organs or to directly move a deadly virus into your bloodstream because he's ticked off.

If sickness were, in fact, the direct result of God's judgment, would we not expect to see some connection between disease and the sins of the flesh? Wouldn't liars, for example, develop more cancer? The proud suffer more car accidents? The sexually immoral have more strokes? The greedy have more kids with birth defects? Spouse-beaters have more heart attacks? As a medical doctor I have treated without partiality God's saints and the Devil's henchmen; I have seen the moral die or become severely disabled from freak medical complications while the immoral "miraculously" survive almost certain death, and I don't see any significant connection or links in general between such sins and sickness.[7]

Let me share some interesting medical data with you on the issue. If you are one of the 60 percent of Americans who are obese or overweight,[8] you are at increased risk for heart disease, stroke, diabetes, and certain cancers (these diseases constitute four out of the top six causes of death in the United States). Approximately three hundred thousand Americans die every year from weight-related causes.[9] Now, I ask, is this God's judgment on everyone who consumes too many calories in their diet? Is this

WHY DOESN'T GOD STOP EVIL?

God's wrath raining down on those who eat one too many Krispy Kreme doughnuts?

What about genetic defects? Defects in single genes are known to be responsible for more than three thousand diseases.[10] Several disorders can be linked to more than one gene, including such diseases as cancer, type two diabetes, asthma, and heart disease. Even autism, attention-deficit hyperactivity disorder (ADHD), and mild mental and reading disabilities are known to be caused in some circumstances by complex modes of inheritance.[11] You might be surprised to learn that chromosomal abnormalities are found in more than half of all first trimester miscarriages.[12]

Our genes, environment, and lifestyles—not God's direct judgment—are responsible for the vast number of diseases we suffer. God may have permitted defective genes (e.g., those linked to breast cancer) to arise in your family tree five, ten, or fifteen generations ago by direct transfer, mutation, or deletion. And in permitting such, God would have known that you would inherit this malfunctioning gene some one hundred or more years later and subsequently fall ill. But again, your sickness was *permitted* by God—not directly *caused* by God because he was getting back at you for something you did.

The human race is united in that we share at least 99.9 percent of our genetic code with our fellow humans—regardless of skin color. Doesn't this make sense as we are all slaves under the same law of sin (see Rom. 8:10, 23)?[13] Doesn't it make sense that we would all similarly age and die? Doesn't it seem logical that we would all be vulnerable to the host of diseases brought about by the fall of mankind back in the garden of Eden? Doesn't it seem natural that the more we age, the more our bodies break down, and the greater the chances we will be sick? God is simply allowing the law of sin to run its due course—to permit the natural consequences of man's original sin to play out in the human race. If you or a loved one has fallen ill, it is highly unlikely that God is punishing you for something you stole, something you smoked, something you said years ago, or something you failed to do.

Jesus' disciples, who had little understanding of genetics, came across a man born blind from birth:

> His disciples asked him, "Rabbi, who sinned, this man or his
> parents, that he was born blind?" "Neither this man nor his
> parents sinned," said Jesus, "but this happened so that the
> work of God might be displayed in his life." (John 9:2–3)

Jesus didn't jump into a lecture on the human genome, but he did tell his followers that this blindness wasn't the result of any specific sin committed by the man (in the womb) or his parents. Just as God allowed this blindness for his glory, God permits sickness in general to satisfy his justice according to the moral laws he has enacted. Sickness is usually *not* justice for any specific sin we've committed, but rather justice for sin in general, stemming back to the garden of Eden. God tells us in Romans 3:23, "For all have sinned and fall short of the glory of God." When justice is served and evil restrained, God's sovereignty, holiness, and moral law are upheld. And in the end, more glory is duly brought to God's righteous and hallowed name.

In the case above, God permitted the sickness so that Jesus' power and mercy might be displayed in the healing of this man, bringing even more glory to God in the big picture of life (see John 9:3, 6–33).

PROVOKING THE WHIRLWIND

> When tempted, no one should say, "God is tempting me."
> For God cannot be tempted by evil, nor does he tempt any-
> one; but each one is tempted when, by his own evil desire,
> he is dragged away and enticed. Then, after desire has con-
> ceived, it gives birth to sin; and sin, when it is full-grown,
> gives birth to death. (James 1:13–15)

"Indeed, much of the heartache for which God is often blamed results from old-fashioned sin," writes the experienced and popular psychologist, Dr. James Dobson.[14] Going a step further, C. S. Lewis attaches a figure: At least 80 percent of mankind's suffering, Lewis maintains, arises from the foolishness, selfishness, and wickedness of the human race.[15] Dr. Charles Stanley guesses, "60 to 70 percent of the people I counsel are suffering from the consequences of their own sin or the sin of another."[16] Often our world reaps what it sows, then turns around and blames God for the whirlwind.

I remember receiving an e-mail a few years back from Linda,[†] a heartbroken widow and mother whom I know quite well. In the e-mail she openly shared with me the burdensome trials she was enduring on account of the bad choices her sons had made. She knew her troubles stemmed directly from her children's immoral actions, yet I could sense that she harbored the universal question in the back of her mind, "Why me, God?"

Her life was a soap opera nightmare. Her grown sons, and some of their girlfriends and ex-wives, battled such vices as alcoholism, illicit drug use, and violent acts of aggression, leading to charges of driving while impaired, assault, and drug use. One son was serving a lengthy prison term. Another had split up with his girlfriend and was trying to regain custody of his children from his previous marriage. Linda was left to pay expensive medical and legal bills for fights and criminal charges incurred by her wayward sons. She was also forced to look after their financial and private affairs, make payments on their loans, fight for court appeals, copetition for one son's joint custody of his children, and in the midst of all this turmoil, try to protect her grandchildren from the emotional pain and suffering. Linda was literally fighting to keep the pieces of her family together while holding down a full-time job. My heart and prayers immediately went out to this loyal and heartbroken mother, who finished her e-mail with the statement, "I stand on the fact that God never sends more than we can bear."

Perhaps in reading through this story you could truly feel this mother's pain because you've been there yourself. A wayward son or daughter has etched across your heart deep scars that no plastic surgeon could ever remove. You've been hit by one whirlwind after another, leaving you with tears and the demoralizing question, What did I do to deserve that?

But I ask, how long can we continue to sow these sins in our nations and not expect to reap the whirlwind? How long can we dabble

---

[†] The names have been changed.

in alcoholism, illicit drug use, adultery, premarital sex, and pornography, and how long can we allow our hearts to teem with pride, deceit, selfishness, lust, and greed—and not expect to reap the whirlwind of murder, school shootings, messy custody battles, sexually transmitted diseases, extortion, poverty, illiteracy, rape, incest, and broken homes? Living in such a wicked world, why should we be surprised when we get hit by a whirlwind started by someone else? When will we finally get it through our thick skulls that God, the divine obstetrician, is just giving the world exactly what it conceives? Our evil desires give birth to sin, "and sin, when it is full-grown, gives birth to death" (James 1:15).

Back to the worldwide AIDS problem: Can we blame God for the millions of men, women, and children dying around the world each year from AIDS? Can we find fault with God if *we* are the ones who choose *not* to follow the Great Physician's prescribed cure for our evils—as he has so plainly outlined in Scripture? If every person abstained from extramarital sex and drug abuse, incurable diseases such as AIDS and genital herpes would be drastically reduced—becoming almost totally eradicated in less than a century. But we'd rather blame God and doubt his goodness than embrace his cure.

But there are worse things, you might say. Experts estimate that ten million children around the world are currently being forced to work as prostitutes. Approximately half a million children are slaves in Bangladesh. Nearly one hundred million children worldwide call the streets their home and workplace. Millions of children have been killed, maimed, blinded, or brain damaged from wars over the past decade. Each day thirty-five thousand children die from malnutrition and preventable diseases.[17] If God is sovereign, how can he allow these evils and all their horrible consequences? What does that say about his goodness?

Obviously there are no easy answers. But let's just consider one of these questions: How can God allow millions of people to starve to death every year? Droughts and floods ("acts of God") certainly cause mass starvation, but here are some additional causes of food shortages that maybe you're not aware of: widespread corruption and bribery, illegal drug trafficking, greed, violence, AIDS, land acquisitions, land reform, political turmoil, wars, mismanagement of government food reserves, turning away of possibly genetically altered food from Western countries, unethical exploitation of natural resources, low respect for human rights and life, inadequate international support, and indifference to crime with resultant injustice, regional strife, and civil conflict.[18] Solomon must have observed similar problems in his day, because he wrote, "A poor man's field may produce abundant food, but injustice sweeps it away" (Prov. 13:23). The problem of famine and disease in underdeveloped countries is a complex and multifactorial problem that is, admittedly, due in part to God's curse on the ground, stemming back to man's original sin. But I believe that humanity's foolish actions—injustice and sin in the present—are responsible for far more of the deaths seen in famine than those caused from the divine "thorns and thistles" curse. If mankind wants to point the finger at God, blaming him for cursing the land from Adam's original sin and predisposing the land to famine, more fingers will be pointing back at the accuser for the multitude of blunders in aggravating the problem of famine as listed above. In actual fact, though, all *ten fingers* should be pointed back at humanity because it was because of humankind's sin that God's curses fell in the first place.

Let's turn our focus back to North America. In my practice of medicine, I have cared for dozens of brain-injured patients. Every year in the United States, more than fifty-two thousand people die from traumatic brain injury (TBI); two hundred thousand victims of TBI require hospitalization; and another 1.74 million suffer mild brain injuries. Financially, TBI costs America an estimated four billion dollars a year, which includes lost potential income, medical expenses, and rehabilitation services.

Do you know the number one cause for TBI? Alcohol is the leading cause (directly and indirectly) of traumatic brain injury in the United States. Alcohol is responsible for the severe disability or death of tens of thousands of Americans every year. It is also responsible for flushing billions of "George Washingtons" down the toilet annually.

I remember one TBI patient quite well. He was a father with four young children, a nice guy who tried to mix alcohol with freeway navigation. As you might have guessed, he didn't do so well at the navigating part and ended up on my ward with a mushed brain, being severely confused and agitated, thrashing around in bed, cursing and shouting, and making inappropriate sexual remarks to the nurses. And his visiting children got to see most of it. He eventually did improve somewhat, but he was never the same person his children or wife remembered. The last I heard, he still couldn't hold down a full-time job. His one day of excess drinking cost this man his job, part of his health and mind, and tens of thousands of dollars in lost income for his family. It also cost the American taxpayer tens of thousands of dollars for his medical expenses.

Who can argue with Solomon when he wrote, "Righteousness exalts a nation, but sin is a disgrace to *any* people" (Prov. 14:34 NASB)? Sin is like a bomb exploding. At its core, the person sinning suffers the greatest damage. But of course, the effects of the evil blast spread far beyond, ripping apart families, communities, cities, and eventually entire nations.

Every day millions of sin bombs are set off under God's nose. And every day, the devastation spreads like nuclear fallout, producing a broken and contaminated world ravaged by the horrors of evil.

> Wisdom is better than weapons of war, but one sinner destroys much good. (Eccl. 9:18)

Maybe it's time we finally put aside our pride and filled the prescription the Great Physician has so lovingly written for us in the Scriptures.

WHY DOESN'T GOD STOP EVIL?

*Constantly choosing the lesser of
two evils is still choosing evil.*[1]

—JERRY GARCIA
MUSICIAN, SINGER (1942–1995)

4
SPILLING THE GOODS ON EVIL

Perhaps you've been thinking to yourself, "I kind of understand God's natural justice in permitting us to reap what we sow. But why doesn't our loving heavenly Father limit evil by preventing us from actually doing the sowing? If God is all-powerful and holy, why doesn't he limit evil by removing the horse before it even has a chance to bust out of the gate? Why doesn't the great judge of the universe tie up, paralyze, or kill, the pedophile before he or she has a chance to murder an innocent child? Why didn't God stop the terrorists on September 11 before they killed thousands of people?"

The common response to these irksome thorns in the side of Christians is, "This is just the natural consequence of human free will." Admittedly, this is a good chunk of the answer. But there is also a strong vein of wisdom running throughout God's justice that Christendom has failed to recognize and appreciate.

Before we answer the question about why God doesn't prevent the pedophile from striking, I want to show you that God has definitely been hard at work to limit the amount of evil in our world—even if it doesn't appear so.

WHY DOESN'T GOD STOP EVIL?

ENOUGH IS ENOUGH!

After Adam and Eve sinned, the hundreds of years leading up to the flood revealed the true potential of man. "The LORD saw how great man's wickedness on the earth had become, and that every inclination of the thoughts of his heart was only evil all the time" (Gen. 6:5). It is possible that pagan teachings had widely propagated the falsehood that "immortality was achieved by immorality."[2] The more wicked one was, the longer he or she would live.

As a result, the world quickly became a cesspool of debauchery. If weapons of mass destruction had existed in Noah's day, God likely wouldn't have needed to send a flood to destroy as many as three billion wicked citizens—they would have probably destroyed themselves with a nuclear bomb or germ warfare.

Why did God allow the wickedness to build up to such staggering levels? I wonder if our ageless God was looking ahead on his personal time line to the humanists who would infect the human race with their sham philosophy: "Man is basically a good creature. We are all born virtuous and good. Everyone should nourish this goodness."

I think God is saying to humanists (who incidentally don't believe in the Genesis record), "You think mankind is good, do you? Look at the evil that explodes when I withhold my restraining influence!" God gave the human race in Noah's day an opportunity to display all the "good" that was within them ... yet mankind failed the test miserably and tragically (see Gen. 6:3). The malicious race of people may have believed that the more wicked they were, the longer they'd live. "As it is written: 'There is no one righteous, not even one'" (Rom. 3:10; cf. Ps. 14:1–3).

God said, "Enough is enough! I've demonstrated far more patience and mercy than these people warrant." And with that he sent a worldwide flood that wiped out almost every living creature from the face of the earth. He also executed a host of other measures over time to restrain evil on those who would repopulate his creation.

Here is a sneak peek at how God has kept a lid on evil down through the ages:

SPILLING THE GOODS ON EVIL

1. *God shortened the human lifespan.* Before the flood, mankind was living upward of 900 years (Adam lived to be 930). After the flood, though, the human lifespan gradually decreased. Noah's son Shem lived to be 600, Shem's son Arphaxad 438 years, followed by his distant descendants Peleg (239 years), Abraham (175), Isaac (180), Jacob (147), Moses (120), and Joshua (110). Two medical specialists, experts on aging, recently wrote in a medical journal that our "'maximum' lifespan can be estimated to be approximately 120 years."[3] Another expert, Robert Lanza, medical director of Advanced Cell Technology in Worcester, MA, says, "Humans hit a wall at 120 years."[4] We get angry with God if we don't live to be eighty or ninety. But back in Noah's day, dying at ninety would have been like dying at fifteen today. This shortening of our lifespan by God took care of the "immortality is achieved by immorality" nonsense (see Ps. 90:10). Because people aged quicker, they were probably sicker, likely from more DNA defects allowed by God. The healthier a person is, and the longer one lives, the greater the magnitude of pride causing one to rebel against God—just as it happened with disastrous consequences in Noah's day.

2. *God instituted government (Gen. 9:5–6).* Orderly human law was needed to discourage, punish, and thwart evil. Think of the chaotic bloodbath that would ensue today without the laws of our land and the police and court systems to enforce it. "The noose, the guillotine, the firing squad, the gas chamber, the electric chair, as well as the sword, the gun, the rifle, the cannon, and missiles stand behind the stability of a civilization—because people are killers."[5] Even an atheist-communist government results in less national evil than no government at all (a state of anarchy).

WHY DOESN'T GOD STOP EVIL?

3. *God scattered the nations (Gen. 11:1–9).* Our triune God scattered the nations at the Tower of Babel by giving each nation a unique language. This successfully divided the people into smaller groups that could move away and more easily set up some form of human government. It also prevented the nations from banding together with proud hearts to implement wickedly idolatrous schemes.

4. *God executed judgment on wicked nations.* In addition to the flood, God poured down fire on the evil Sodomites (Gen. 19:24) and used the Israelites to wipe out most of the wicked Canaanite nations. "There has never been a greater war for a greater cause. The battle of Waterloo decided the fate of Europe, but this series of contests in far-off Canaan decided the fate of the world."[6] By wiping out wicked cities and nations, God spared the world from their wicked influence.

5. *God permitted the existence of unstable weather systems (Gen. 9:13–14).* It is possible that before the flood, there was no rain and no clouds (Gen. 2:5), just a heavy nightly dew that watered the earth. For some reason, the flood likely wrought havoc on our weather systems, allowing for rainstorms and droughts. It's likely that tornadoes, hurricanes, and earthquakes started around this time. How does this keep evil in check? The uncertainty in our weather patterns has always been an impetus for mankind to turn to God— at least in our thoughts—hence the term, *acts of God.* Natural disasters are naturally humbling to the human race—helping to break down the human wall of pride and reduce evil in general.

6. *God gave us his law (Ex. 20:1–17).* Almost a thousand years after the flood, God wrote his moral law in stone, clearly defining the moral statutes that he expected mankind to follow.

7. *God has permitted the global expansion of false religions.*
   Though God hates idolatry, I believe he has allowed
   many religions to flourish in the past two thousand
   years to help curb the flagrant manifestations of evil. (If
   humans weren't worshipping some other god, we'd
   likely be worshipping ourselves—which is every bit as
   bad; see 2 Tim. 3:1–5). I believe these religions have
   done little, however, to curb the *hidden* sins of the
   heart (see Col. 2:23). For instance, most religions will
   persuade us not to kill, but humanity will continue to
   foster hate in the heart. Religion, for the most part, is
   just another formal structure of government, complete
   with a catalog of moral rules that aids in keeping the
   visible manifestations of evil in check. Those who will
   not submit to the one true God of the universe will
   usually submit to some kind of human-devised legalis-
   tic code that restrains actions but does not transform
   the heart.

8. *God sent his Holy Spirit down to the world to convict
   people of sin (John 16:7–11).* Actually, it is only by the
   Holy Spirit's power that we are able to grasp the truth
   in our broken state and submit to God (John 6:61–65;
   14:16–17, 26). And as believers in Christ's church,
   whom Christ calls the "salt of the earth" (Matt. 5:13),
   we are also part of God's instruments in reducing evil by
   being a shining light in a very dark world (Phil. 2:15).

Of course, God's judgments are not just about keeping evil in
check. What was God thinking when he sent the worldwide flood in
Noah's day? The same thing he was thinking when he brought down his
curses in the garden of Eden: *justice.* "Righteousness and justice are the
foundation of his throne" we read in Psalm 97:2b. Yes, God's wrath,
curses, and judgments stem from his altogether holy and just being.
But God's justice is also firmly rooted in his matchless wisdom.

Let's say we spill the "goods" on the consequences of evil.

WHY DOESN'T GOD STOP EVIL?

WHY NOT JUST "PULL A TOM CRUISE"?

As you can see, God *has* done much to curb the wild horses of evil in the human heart—much more than we realize. These are the "footprints" of God in our world that most believers fail to spy. Without the Almighty restraining evil to this degree, it's very doubtful that any of us would be alive today. Who do you think has been responsible up to this point in history for keeping evil fingers off the nuclear warhead launch buttons? Who do you think is protecting the military storage of the deadly smallpox virus in America and Russia from terrorists? Who do you think is thwarting the terrorists in their attempts to build and detonate nuclear bombs in the Western world? If you think about it, you can see that God has restrained far more evil than that which he has allowed to trickle through (see Ps. 76:10; 2 Thess. 2:7). And he has done so mainly by restraining sin at the level of the heart.

But he doesn't stop everything. And that brings us back to the question of why he doesn't strike down the pedophile before he or she has a chance to strike. Wouldn't that be the wise thing for God to do?

In the futuristic movie, *Minority Report*, Tom Cruise played Washington, DC's best "pre-cognitive" cop who, with the help of psychics, could see into the future and bust the murderers before they had a chance to murder. Most of us can't figure out why God doesn't "pull a Tom Cruise" and do the same thing.

There are stories in Scripture, such as the story of Joseph and his brothers, where God fit evil perfectly into his flawless plan. But I believe there are other explanations behind why God allows the tragic consequences of evil to unfold in our world.

First, God's goodness, fairness, grace, and mercy stop him from killing all of us. When people ask, "Why couldn't God have prevented this criminal from raping a teenager, or killing a neighbor, or planting a bomb?" I often wonder what they expect God to do. For instance, what about the man who keeps beating his wife? Should God instantly paralyze the guy from the neck down to prevent any further abuse? Should God strike him down on the spot with a heart attack? Or allow the flesh-eating disease to take one of his arms? Some of you reading this would answer, "Yes! Give the creep exactly what he deserves!"

What would happen if God gave the rest of us what *we* deserve? God abhors the sins of pride and lying (roughly 30 percent of job applications contain outright lies or "inflated" info).[7] If God were to paralyze, maim, or kill the spouse-beater or pedophile, what do you think he should do to those of us who relentlessly keep building up the walls of pride and deceit in our hearts? Should he not also kill or maim us to prevent the conceit that is just as evil in his sight as beating one's spouse (see Prov. 6:16–19)? If God were to fairly give us "all that we deserve," the only creatures left to exist on the planet would be the four-, six-, and eight-legged kind (plus birds, fish, and centipedes).

The servant Friday, in his broken English, inquisitively asked Robinson Crusoe one day, "But if God much strong, much might as the devil, why God no kill the devil so make him no more do wicked?" Crusoe reflected for a moment, then replied, "You may as well ask, why does God not kill you and me when we do wicked things that offend Him."[8]

Paul E. Little, who spoke at more than 180 college campuses throughout America, Europe, and Latin America, before he died in a tragic car accident at forty-six years of age, wrote this:

> If God were to stamp out evil today, He would do a *complete* job.... His action would be complete and would have to include our lies and personal impurities, our lack of love, and our failure to do good. Suppose God were to decree that at midnight tonight *all* evil would be removed from the universe—who of us would still be here after midnight?[9]

Second, the consequences of evil limit outward acts of sin and encourage godly actions. If there weren't some observable connection between what a person sowed and what the same person reaped, would we not just throw up our hands and exclaim, "What does it matter? If I'm wise and do well, I suffer. And if I'm foolish and do bad, I suffer. What motivation do I have to obey God's moral laws?"

WHY DOESN'T GOD STOP EVIL?

The horrific consequences of evil often bring change. School shootings cause us to pay more attention to how we raise our children. Thirty-eight percent of parents recently surveyed reported that they are trying to shelter their children from school violence by becoming more actively involved in their children's schools. Almost half of parents say they pay more attention to their children's behavior and whereabouts now than before the school shootings.[10] How many millions of children have benefited from parents taking more of an interest in their physical and spiritual well-being? Who knows? Maybe more adults were hit with a greater sense of the preciousness and privilege of life after the Columbine school shootings, thereby helping to decrease the number of abortions.

Third, and most importantly, the consequences of evil limit acts of sin in the heart. This truth is absolutely crucial for us to understand. The brokenness we see all around us—sickness, AIDS, earthquakes, wars, murder, and death—all of this brokenness works back to decrease the amount of evil in our hearts (refer to the diagram "Consequences of Evil" on p. 47), not only in the hearts of those suffering a particular tragedy, but for the hundreds, or perhaps millions, of others looking on. We read in Isaiah 26:9, "When your judgments come upon the earth, the people of the world learn righteousness." The brokenness we observe in our world chips away at the hidden sins in our hearts— whether we're believers or unbelievers. This results in less sin overall, to the benefit of mankind and the glory of God.

Let me explain as best I can: The existence of sexually transmitted diseases, such as AIDS, herpes, and gonorrhea, serves to deter outward promiscuous sexual activity, but it also helps to decrease the lust in our hearts. If you rule out the possibility of sex before marriage because you are afraid of contracting an incurable sexually transmitted disease, you will be far less inclined to lust after someone by making plans in your heart as to how you will go about getting that person into bed. Therefore, the consequences of evil, such as AIDS, help to keep a damper on lust and decrease the amount of promiscuous sex and prostitution (and thus decrease the incidence of divorce and the number of broken homes). God abhors the sins of the heart above all else.

Here's another example: Every year, approximately fourteen hundred young American adults, aged eighteen to twenty-four, are killed in alcohol-related accidents.[11] Now, Princess Diana was outside this age-range, but just after her death a television producer phoned Philip Yancey and asked, "Can you appear on our show? We want you to explain how God could possibly allow such a terrible accident." Yancey quickly responded, "Could it have had something to do with a drunk driver going ninety miles an hour in a narrow tunnel? How, exactly, was God involved?"[12]

Observing all the tragic alcohol-related deaths from car, boating, and snowmobile accidents results in less alcohol abuse overall in adults and teenagers than would be the case otherwise. This, in turn, results in fewer cases of rape, vandalism, trauma, divorce, spousal abuse, and child abuse. I've spoken with many young people who totally abstain from alcohol because they've seen the devastating effects of alcoholism as it ripped through their family and communities. But most importantly, the tragic consequences of alcohol help to scour our hearts of the wretchedness of pride.

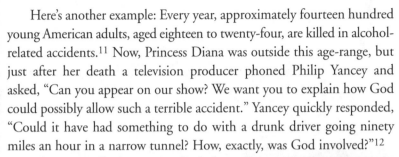

SUPPOSE GOD WERE TO DECREE THAT AT MIDNIGHT TONIGHT *ALL* EVIL WOULD BE REMOVED FROM THE UNIVERSE— WHO OF US WOULD STILL BE HERE AFTER MIDNIGHT?

Imagine if all the parents in America were to collectively equip their vehicles with high-tech computers that would take over control of the car if their teenagers were to get behind the wheel while intoxicated. By removing the consequences of drinking and driving, would this not encourage the child to drink even more, leaving the door wide open for horrific consequences? "Who cares what God expects from me? I'm just going to get drunk and party on, dude." When an individual believes he or she is immune to such disasters, the pride meter goes through the roof. The consequences of alcohol abuse, therefore, serve to limit evil—particularly pride.

WHY DOESN'T GOD STOP EVIL?

In addition, "chance" tragedies, such as volcanic eruptions, ice storms, wildfires, floods, sickness, carjackings, drunk-driver accidents, and any form of death, also take a huge bite out of our selfishness and pride. They serve as hundreds of post-it notes stuck on our minds, telling us, "You are not in control of your destiny." For the most part, we can't predict whether we'll be hit by a car tomorrow, lose our home in a fire, or drop dead from meningitis or a heart attack. This uncertainty acts like a powerful water cannon, helping to control the flames of pride in our hearts.

Perhaps you've been hit with a particular chance tragedy. Maybe your house burned down; maybe it was flooded out or destroyed in a tornado or hurricane; perhaps your child or spouse developed cancer and became deathly ill. Undoubtedly, God does sometimes use some horrible events—such "burning bushes"—to get our attention if we are his children and straying spiritually. But I believe the majority of such events fall into the "nothing personal" category.

God is saying in effect, "Hey, I'm not directly punishing you for a specific sin you committed. And I still love you every bit as much. All I'm doing is allowing the natural consequences of evil, set in motion since the garden of Eden, to play out. Because mankind as a whole has sinned against me, justice dictates that everyone is susceptible to the worldly penalties according to the law of sin. No one is immune."

You might be the godliest saint in your community; and you might question why God allowed a particular tragedy to come your way. Remember that not even the greatest saints deserve anything from God (see Rom. 3:23). But think of the hundreds or thousands of others who, after observing your particular tragedy, are yanked back to their spiritual senses: "Wow! This was a good family and look what happened to them! This same tragedy could have easily happened to me. Maybe it's time I got my spiritual priorities right in life." You may not be struggling too much with pride, but your tragedy could very well help to tear down the skyscrapers of pride in the hearts of hundreds or perhaps thousands of others looking on.

Now I ask you, Why doesn't God "pull a Tom Cruise" and bust the criminals before they have a chance to strike? What is God thinking when he allows the horrible evils of murder, assault, and rape every day? What is God thinking when he allows the loss of life from tragedies such as earthquakes, tornadoes, and killer viruses? God knows all too well that the heart is the sole breeding ground for every imaginable evil (see Mark 7:20–23). If God were to supernaturally protect us from all the consequences of evil, our hearts would be so utterly proud, lustful, greedy, selfish, and hateful, we'd make the citizens of Sodom and Gomorrah look like angelic choirboys.

Not everyone, of course, sees things this way. I don't know about you, but I'm starting to get a little tired of all the televangelists who jump on the "judgment bandwagon" every time a tornado, wildfire, earthquake, flood, or terrorist attack occurs: "This is clearly God's judgment on America!" they declare to millions of viewers and radio listeners.

Here's something for you to ponder in bed tonight. Could God's sovereign plan in allowing the consequences of evil to surface in America actually be evidence that he really cares about the spiritual welfare of the country? Could God be allowing all these natural and human-devised tragedies in an effort to stem the future tide of evil in the hearts of Americans—thereby raising the level of spiritual wisdom and making the country a better place in which to live? Are we looking at all these tragedies from the right perspective?

In Canada, for instance, a recent Ipsos-Reid poll found that of those Canadians whose faith in God had increased over the years, approximately 23 percent attributed their faith makeover to "natural disasters or wars." Thirty-four percent said their faith in God increased because of a "personal or family illness."[13] Overall though, Canada has fewer natural disasters and terrorist attacks and proportionately less crime than the United States. Is this one reason why Canada has a smaller percentage of born-again Christians than America? Does God use natural disasters and crime, not only to decrease the amount of puffed-up pride in a nation, but also in some way as part of his "drawing process" in supernaturally bringing a sinner to genuine repentance (see John 6:44)? God doesn't necessarily *have* to use such calamities for these reasons, but he can.

WHY DOESN'T GOD STOP EVIL?

We see similar trends across the Atlantic ocean: At the turn of the millennium, America had approximately 50 percent more climatic disasters than Europe.[14] Around the same time, America had a higher homicide rate than any Western European country.[15] Is it just a coincidence then that Europe is spiritually cold, while the United States has probably the highest percentage of genuine born-again Christians in any nation besides China? Just imagine the positive impact that calamities and misfortunes may have had on Americans' faith in God.

Never ever forget: "Man looks at the outward appearance, but the LORD looks at the heart" (1 Sam. 16:7b). It is the heart God is most concerned with. And if he can use the consequences of evil to stem the tide of evil in our hearts, he'll do it.

The brokenness we experience on earth dramatically helps to decrease the not-so-secret sins of the heart, increase true spiritual wisdom, and direct our focus back to God. Here is just another amazing example of how justice and wisdom are inseparable in God's finely balanced character. And here is another example of how much God cares about the spiritual welfare of humanity.

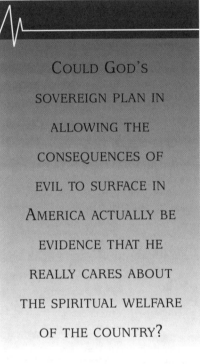

COULD GOD'S SOVEREIGN PLAN IN ALLOWING THE CONSEQUENCES OF EVIL TO SURFACE IN AMERICA ACTUALLY BE EVIDENCE THAT HE REALLY CARES ABOUT THE SPIRITUAL WELFARE OF THE COUNTRY?

On a street corner in downtown Oakland, an old woman sold pretzels for $1.00 each. Every afternoon a well-dressed man would hurry by and toss a dollar bill in her cup without taking a pretzel. One day as he rushed off yet again, the woman shouted to him, "Just a minute, sir!"

"I know, I know," he said. "You're wondering why it is I pay you but never take a pretzel."

"No," the woman answered, "I wanted to tell you the price has gone up to $1.50."[1]

5

WHERE WAS GOD ON SEPTEMBER 11?

Since the horrific tragedy that took the lives of nearly three thousand people on September 11, 2001, the question has been asked over and over again, "Where was God when the hijackers struck?" The tragedy that shocked the world shook the hearts of hundreds of millions across the globe. In my living room I watched the CNN footage in horror as the second plane struck the towers … then in utter disbelief as the towers came crashing down.

How could God allow a catastrophe as horrible as this to happen?

The questions and accusations flew. Mixed in with our grief was an apparent need to place blame. First God was blamed. Then the FBI. Then the CIA. Then Osama Bin Laden. Then the Devil. Then Canada (even though none of the hijackers entered the United States from that country). Then George Bush. Then we came back full circle to questioning and attacking God. It seems that we are born predisposed to blaming somebody, some country, or something—otherwise, those irksome questions in our subconscious would frustrate us toward the brink of insanity.

WHY DOESN'T GOD STOP EVIL?

Everywhere I go these days I hear of people who can't understand how God can allow such horrific tragedies to occur. How can a God who is supposed to be so good allow such evil in his creation?

Because so many questions concerning God have surfaced since the tragedy, I thought it might be helpful if we tackled the tough question, What was God thinking when he allowed the terrorists to strike on 9/11? Though I hope that such a disaster never strikes again, this may be a question that will continue to surface and resonate throughout the decades to come.

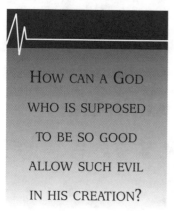

HOW CAN A GOD WHO IS SUPPOSED TO BE SO GOOD ALLOW SUCH EVIL IN HIS CREATION?

Soon after the World Trade Center towers came crashing down there was a rush to interview religious leaders across the country. At first, their consoling and comforting words were sought for those grieving over the heartrending loss of a father, mother, brother, sister, spouse, or child. Then came the inevitable questions that demanded not-so-easy answers. The responses varied considerably, from Anne Graham Lotz's statement that God was only being a perfect "gentleman" by backing out of America's national life as requested by its citizens and courts to Jerry Falwell's adamant proclamation that God was raining down judgment on America specifically for all its sins of abortion, adultery, pornography, and homosexuality. Astonishingly, Kenneth Copeland claimed that it wasn't God's judgment on Americans at all—but on Muslims—because of what the American military would later do.[2]

How do we know what God was *really* thinking?

Perhaps, like me, you received a widely circulating e-mail a few days after the ghastly attack explaining where God was on September 11, 2001. "God was busy saving lives," was the point pounded home in the e-mail. God was there in the Twin Towers getting people out quickly. God didn't allow the hijackers to fly the planes into the towers when thousands more people would have been inside. The Almighty kept the number of passengers low on all four hijacked flights so that fewer people would die. "Miraculously," numerous workers were late or sick that day and never made it to work. Without God's divine intervention, wrote the anonymous author, thousands of more people would have been killed.

Whenever a tragedy strikes, the first thing a believer does is instinctively think, "It could have been much, much worse without God around." For God to just sit back and twiddle his thumbs in such a parade of evil would be unimaginable to most of us. But how many deaths did God really prevent?

It must be remembered that the terrorists had spent years planning their extremely well-coordinated and methodically executed attacks on 9/11. Even though they knew that only about thirty-five thousand of the fifty thousand plus people who worked at the Twin Towers would be at their desks before 9:00 a.m., and that only a fraction of the two hundred thousand people (almost half of them tourists) who regularly passed through the buildings each day would be inside, they still chose early morning flights. Why? Because their primary goal was not to kill as many people as possible but to hit all four highly visible American landmarks.[3]

You see, in 2001 nearly one in four commercial flights were delayed by more than fifteen minutes.[4] Maybe you don't know this, but the further along in the day a flight is scheduled to depart, the greater the chances it will be delayed. The terrorists knew this, so they commandeered transcontinental flights with thousands of gallons of fuel *early in the morning*—all scheduled to depart within twenty-two minutes of each other. To succeed with the ghastly plan, all four planes had to be right on time. The terrorists couldn't risk even one flight being ten minutes late because they knew that once the planes started hitting their targets, the F-16 fighter jets would be in the air and all flights would be grounded.

The terrorists had done their homework well. They even purposely chose flights with few passengers aboard so that the chances of the four or five hijackers being overpowered by the passengers on each flight would be minimized. Only 247 crew and passengers (not counting the nineteen hijackers) were on board the four large Boeing 757 and 767 aircraft. In fact, more firefighters on the ground (about 350) lost their lives on 9/11 than passengers and crew in the air.

WHY DOESN'T GOD STOP EVIL?

And what about all those amazing stories we heard of people who unknowingly escaped death when they called in sick, were late, or missed their trains? Didn't God providentially work circumstances out to save certain people? I'm sure he did. Yet on any given workday there were, statistically speaking, probably hundreds of people out of the fifty thousand who were late, sick, or unable to make it to work for one reason or another. September 11, 2001, was likely just another regular workday with hundreds of people not in their offices when they should have been.

Now, the heroic acts of the passengers and crew aboard United Flight 93 did save lives. And maybe God had something to do with keeping the cell phones working on the plane as passengers learned from loved ones of the tragic events unfolding in New York. As a result, the airliner crashed in a field in rural Pennsylvania instead of the Capitol building or the White House. Lives were definitely saved by the heroes aboard Flight 93, but people were already being evacuated from the Washington landmarks, and politicians were already huddled in bunkers when the airliner was still in the air. (Admittedly, God may have directly intervened to keep the joint chiefs of staff safe in the northeast side of the Pentagon when American Airlines Flight 77 hit the other side of the structure.)

It seems apparent from intercepted communiqué that the terrorists never expected the towers to come crashing down. The towers were initially built to withstand a direct hit from a jetliner. The overall destruction and the total number of deaths, about three thousand, were beyond the expectations of even the terrorists. Did God significantly limit the number of casualties on 9/11? It doesn't appear so. In fact, the major airlines' dismal track record for on-time flights was probably what ultimately saved tens of thousands of more people from being killed.

FIRE AND BRIMSTONE?

So if God didn't significantly limit the number of deaths, then 9/11 must have been God's judgment on America, right?

WHERE WAS GOD ON SEPTEMBER 11?

It's obviously impossible for us to crawl inside the mind of God to figure out what was going through his head the day the terrorists struck. "Who has known the mind of the Lord?" challenges the apostle Paul (Rom. 11:34). Who are we to say exactly what God's intention was that dreadful day? How can we possibly know just how the tragedy fit perfectly into his most beautiful mosaic? And how can we, the clay, stand up and declare that what happened on September 11 definitely was or was not the direct judgment of the Potter?

Though we can't know for sure why God allowed the hijackers to strike, I believe the Scriptures do offer us some valuable clues. To those who argue that this definitely *was* God's fire and brimstone raining down upon America for its moral bankruptcy, I ask (with all due respect to those who lost their lives), How many people have to die before it becomes officially "God's judgment"? Fifty? One hundred? One thousand? Three thousand? Is God's direct judgment raining down on the nation every time an American life is lost? Is every train derailment, freeway multicar pile-up, plane crash, gas explosion, or heat stroke caused from a blistering heat wave, God's unequivocal judgment?

Now, please, don't go away with the impression that I'm making light in any way of those who lost their lives on September 11. What happened that dark day was a devastating catastrophe. But if we want some answers to what happened we must be prepared to look at the tragedy from God's perspective.

Understanding where I'm coming from then, do you know how many Americans die every week? Approximately fifty thousand! Every day, more than seven thousand Americans die from various causes. That means, that on September 11, 2001, more than twice as many Americans died from nonterrorist related causes as died as a result of the hijackers. "We are more comfortable when people die one by one," adds MacArthur. "It makes the fact of death easier to ignore."[5]

Do you still think the terrorist attacks were judgment day on America? Here are three reasons why the tragic events were most likely *not* the firsthand judgment of God:

One, is America any more wicked than any other country? Are abortions, extortion, murders, incest, and homosexuality isolated to

WHY DOESN'T GOD STOP EVIL?

only America? Let me also remind you that, with the possible exception of the underground church in China, America has the greatest number of genuine believers of any other country in the world. Moreover, we are living in the age (God's parenting strategy) of grace (see John 1:17; Rom. 6:14) while God's wrath is currently on the disobedient (see Col. 3:6).[6] For the most part, God is storing up his wrath to be unleashed during the tribulation period and on the final judgment day (see Eccl. 3:17; Rom. 2:5; 2 Thess. 1:7–9; Rev. 6–19).

Two, in the Old Testament, when God poured down his judgment on a nation, city, or group of people, almost always a sizeable proportion of the population was affected. (The cities of Sodom and Gomorrah were entirely destroyed; only eight people survived the flood; and almost all the Canaanites were killed by the Israelites.) Furthermore, I know of no examples in New Testament history where God judged entire nations suddenly, unless you want to include the slaughter and bondage of the Jewish nation at the hands of the Romans about AD 70. So, although the tragedy of 9/11 is significant, relatively speaking, three thousand people dying does not constitute a sizable proportion by God's past judgment standards.

Three, ask yourself, "Why did the Muslim extremists attack America in the first place?" Listen to the Al-Qaeda videotapes and the answer is clear. Bin Laden said it himself several times. The primary reason America was targeted is because of America's activities in the Middle East—particularly in helping the nation of Israel. (I'm sure Russia is grateful that the Jews haven't flown any airliners into the Kremlin as revenge for Russia's history in helping the Arab nations.)

Can we draw a rough comparison between the disaster on September 11 and the persecution of Christians who follow God's ways? Does God promise believers that no evil will befall us if we serve Christ? Just the opposite. We are told that we will be persecuted for doing right (see John 15:20); yet we will also be spiritually blessed by God's favor. The Lord addressed the infant nation of Israel: "I will bless those who bless you, and whoever curses you I will curse" (Gen. 12:3). I think it's quite obvious to much of the world that God has blessed America throughout the years.

WHERE WAS GOD ON SEPTEMBER 11?

Yes, God abhors America's sins more than we can possibly imagine. But when we take everything into consideration, we might come to realize that what happened on September 11 was primarily the result of what America was doing right, rather than what America was doing wrong.

YOU DIDN'T ANSWER MY QUESTION: WHERE WAS GOD ON 9/11?

Before you become too swollen with national pride if you are an American, let's finish our discussion. On the CBS *Early Show*, Jane Clayson asked Anne Graham Lotz, the daughter of Billy and Ruth Graham, how a good God could have allowed something as awful as this to happen.

Anne explained:

> I would say also for several years now Americans in a sense have shaken their fist at God and said, God, we want you out of our schools, our government, our business, we want you out of our marketplace. And God, who is a gentleman, has just quietly backed out of our national and political life, our public life. Removing his hand of blessing and protection.[7]

Ms. Lotz, who is president and executive director of Angel Ministries, hits upon an important truth. And that is, those who do the *least* for God always seem to expect the *most* from God. I mean, forget the fact that we profane God's name every day in our films, curse him in our workplaces, ignore him 363 days a year, pay him lip service only on Christmas and Easter, deride the poor, cheat on our spouses, and murder millions of babies in grotesque abortions (an estimated 234,000 evangelical Christian women in America purposely abort every year),[8] "C'mon God. I *demand* my protection, my comfort, my security—my happy meals!—just like I ordered!"

Though Ms. Lotz politely exposes the world's indifference to the sovereignty, majesty, and holiness of God, I believe her statement reflects somewhat unfairly on God's character. For it might leave some with the wrong impression that God backed away, relinquished control, and took his hands off the whole situation. Or it might leave some with the lingering sense that God is like some snooty teenage girl who's saying, "If you don't invite me to your party, I'm not going to invite you to mine." And God isn't like that.

What was God saying on September 11? I like how John MacArthur put it:

> He's saying, "People, you're going to die, and you don't have control of it. This is a reminder. I give you life. I give you love. I give you happiness. I pour out all the common grace. And make life rich and rewarding and full. I do everything I can. I'm patient. I'm forbearing. I'm merciful. I'm gracious. But once in a while I have to show you a stark illustration of where you're going."[9]

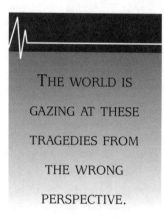

THE WORLD IS GAZING AT THESE TRAGEDIES FROM THE WRONG PERSPECTIVE.

In many ways we're like the woman in the pretzel joke. We instinctively expect God to keep handing over more and more money to our little cardboard "pretzel stand" here on earth. We even raise the price—raise our expectations of God's bountiful blessings. But when God finally does take a pretzel—something that rightfully belongs to him—we grow angry and resentful. We expect God to keep pouring down more and more of his grace and mercy each day, protecting us when we don't deserve it, comforting us when we scoff at his majesty, and blessing us when we ignore him. Then we turn around and suddenly grow bitter when he takes something that only he deserves, something he created.

Imagine that you were the one who had toiled for hours baking the chewy glazed bread, and every afternoon you came by and put a dollar in your salesperson's jar without taking a pretzel? How would you feel if, one day, you decided to take a pretzel, only to have your employee quickly slap your wrist, saying, "Hands off! The price just went up!" How do you think God feels when he, who created us and restrains evil every day to make "life rich and rewarding and full," decides to touch his creation—or allow it to be touched—only to have us snarl, "Hands off, God! You owe us more!"

Who *really* owns the pretzels—and the pretzel stand?

For some reason, we've grabbed hold of the misguided notion that we *deserve* to live. But let me point this out: Adam and Eve didn't deserve to live after they disobeyed God; Noah and his family didn't deserve to be saved on the ark; the children of Israel didn't deserve to live after they began worshipping idols; not one of us living here on earth deserves to be alive at this very moment. If God's justice were the only perfection operating, none of us would exist.

Ironically, then, the world is gazing at these tragedies from the wrong perspective. We should not be asking ourselves why God killed millions of people in the flood. Or why God ordered Joshua to kill thousands of Canaanites. Or why God allowed almost three thousand people to die on September 11. We should be asking, "Why do any of us live?" That is the most baffling question of all. The only reason the firefighters, police officers, parents, spouses, and children who died on 9/11 were alive in the first place was because of God's great love and grace in restraining evil down through the centuries and *not* giving us what we deserve. It is only by the matchless grace of almighty God that any of us are alive today. We are like the young Nigerian man in the story earlier who was complaining that the white miracle doctor didn't give him any life-sustaining "magic seeds." "It's not your right to live," shares MacArthur. "It's God's grace that gives you life."[10]

The classic text for why God allows such calamities to occur is found in Luke 13:1–5. Eighteen "innocent" people were evidently walking along the street one day, and suddenly BOOM!—the tower of Siloam falls on them, killing them all. The disciples apparently asked, or wondered, "Did the tower fall on these people because they were worse sinners than anyone else?" Jesus replied: "Do you think they were more guilty than all the others living in Jerusalem? I tell you, no! But unless you repent, you too will all perish" (vv. 4–5).

WHY DOESN'T GOD STOP EVIL?

When the disciples questioned Jesus as to why this tragedy occurred, did Christ say, "You know, it could have been much worse had God not intervened." Did he say, "The tower fell on these people as a direct judgment for all the abortions, homosexuality, pride, materialism, and adultery going on in your nation?" Did Christ say, "God was only being the perfect 'gentleman' by backing off and giving you what you wanted?" Christ's immediate answer was, "No! But unless you repent, you too will all perish" (v. 5).

> We live under constant mercy so when justice shows up we're shocked. We get so used to grace that we don't understand justice.[11]

"For the wages of sin is death," writes Paul (Rom. 6:23). When your employer hands you your paycheck at the end of the week, your earned wages are paid out to the exact cent. Is your employer a vengeful and malicious tyrant for giving you exactly what you deserve? No. And neither is God for giving people exactly what they deserve—right down to the last "cent." All of us are aging—dying physically on the inside—and will one day be buried or have our ashes scattered. For some of us, God decides to pay us our deserved wages a little earlier than we'd like. Certainly no one can fault God for that.

I don't personally believe that September 11 was God's direct judgment on America for its present sins; rather, I believe it was likely his indirect justice brought about by the natural consequences of evil that he allowed, in part, to help restrain the future hidden sins in our hearts. God allowed the evil in the hijackers' hearts to play out naturally. And the evil consequences—the approximately three thousand people killed—acted like a mighty water cannon to help control the flames of pride and selfishness in all our hearts.

Were those people who died on September 11 punished because they were worse sinners than the rest of us? No. But as Christ so clearly stated, unless we repent of our sins, unless we humbly bow the knee to him and ask for forgiveness for all the pain we've caused him, unless we submissively accept Christ's death on the cross as full payment for the evil that exists at the core of every one of us,[12] then we will suffer spiritual death in hell—something that is far, far worse than physical death here on earth (see Matt. 25:46).

"Where was God on September 11?" many asked. Right where he's always been since the creation of the world: *on his rightful throne and in complete control of absolutely everything.* Every life lost on September 11 in New York, Washington, Pennsylvania, around America, and through-out the world that day, was precious to God. Every one of us is dear to God. And even though America has tried to push the King of kings out of its schools, its government, and its workplaces, God lovingly and stubbornly remains in absolutely every cubic inch of the country.

When the first plane struck the towers that bright sunny morning, God was right there, most likely affirming this to America: "By my grace I have foiled several previous attempts by the terrorists to try and mur-der your loved ones and destroy your beautiful country. But I hate the hidden sins of the heart too much to allow them to escalate and make a mockery of my person. And I care too much about America to allow these future sins—the sins of pride, selfishness, and greed—to eventu-ally destroy your nation. I can't, in my infinite wisdom and love, withhold this natural consequence of evil when I know that it will save America from untold evils to come. Once in a while I must shake you to your spiritual senses to show you where you're heading.

"If you do what is right, America, I will continue to spiritually pros-per you. If you submit your lives to me you will be immeasurably blessed. All I ask is that you turn your hearts around and humbly repent, lest you likewise perish.

"That is all I ask of you."

WHY DOESN'T GOD STOP EVIL?

No king is saved by the size of his army;
no warrior escapes by his great strength.
A horse is a vain hope for deliverance;
despite all its great strength it cannot save.

—PSALM 33:16–17

6

HURRICANE KATRINA:
GOD'S DIVINE AGENDA?

To err is human. To blame someone else is politics.
—US politician, Hubert H. Humphrey

Like September 11, Hurricane Katrina didn't take long to gather up the unwilling contestants for the popular prime-time reality TV show, "The Blame Game." Hurricane Katrina had just left New Orleans and surrounding counties looking, from an aerial view, like a toddler's dismantled Legoland creation in a clogged and smelly bathtub. It was a horrible catastrophe beyond description. Dead bodies floated past stop signs. Those who survived the flood waded or swam through oil, sewage, and miniature islands of garbage in search of food. Mothers, clutching their crying children in their arms, struggled to stay afloat. Rescuers were haunted by the screams of victims trapped inside their attics—unable to break through the roof as the waters continued to rise. Almost overnight, Katrina produced roughly a half million refugees, killed more than a thousand Gulf Coast residents across Louisiana, Mississippi, and Alabama, stole

WHY DOESN'T GOD STOP EVIL?

power from more than a million people, and punched several holes (some nearly the length of a football field) in the levees—making it one of the worst natural disasters in US history.

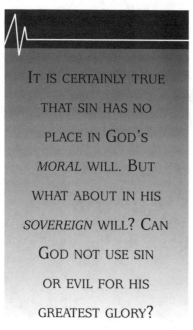

IT IS CERTAINLY TRUE THAT SIN HAS NO PLACE IN GOD'S *MORAL* WILL. BUT WHAT ABOUT IN HIS *SOVEREIGN* WILL? CAN GOD NOT USE SIN OR EVIL FOR HIS GREATEST GLORY?

Obviously, someone had to be blamed for the resulting suffering: Mayor Ray Nagin could only kick himself for relying too much on the federal government; Louisiana's governor, Kathleen Blanco, took full responsibility. And even President Bush admitted that Katrina exposed major problems in the response capability of the government at all levels and took responsibility to the extent that the federal government didn't fully do its job sufficiently.

But was there another contestant missing from the "blame game"? I'm not talking about the ex-FEMA director Michael Brown—I'm talking about God. No one could reasonably blame the president or local officials for the storm itself. After all, it was "an act of God."

So then *was* Hurricane Katrina part of God's divine agenda for residents of the Gulf Coast? And *was* God's sovereign will done on August 29, 2005?

It is certainly true that sin has no place in God's *moral* will. But what about in his *sovereign* will? Can God not use sin or evil for his greatest glory? Don't we read in Proverbs 16:4, "The Lord works out *everything* for his own ends—even the wicked for a day of disaster" (see also Rom. 9:17–23). If God didn't send or allow Hurricane Katrina, then who did? Is there someone more powerful than God who is running our galaxy? Was there someone higher in rank than President Bush who should have taken responsibility for Hurricane Katrina?

Now, some might blame the abhorrent rescue efforts solely on poor leadership. Nancy Gibbs writes in *Time* magazine:

> Katrina was in the cards, forewarned, foreseen and yet still dismissed. That so many officials were caught so unprepared was a failure less of imagination than will.[1]

Could God have planned some big rescue mission but mankind screwed things up royally? Who is to blame, though, if we don't take reasonable measures to protect ourselves from "acts of God"—such as deadly hurricanes? Especially when we know the *exact* day it is coming ashore. Earthquakes and terrorists do not practice "call ahead seating," alerting those in charge as to where and when they will show up. But hurricanes are a different story. America knew in advance that Katrina, an unwelcome guest, was coming for breakfast on Monday August 29, 2005. How many decades did we think New Orleans, resting on prime megahurricane real estate, could "party on, dude" before being hit by a category four or five hurricane?

No matter how the human race acts, God's sovereign will is *always* done on earth, as we discovered earlier from a multitude of Scripture verses. Many believers and nonbelievers, though, don't understand God's will—or his nature. They believe that a great and holy God of love could never be directly responsible for sending a deadly hurricane upon a nation. But God tells us differently in his Word: "I form the light and create darkness, I bring prosperity and create disaster; I, the LORD, do all these things" (Isa. 45:7). We also read, "When a trumpet sounds in a city, do not the people tremble? When disaster comes to a city, has not the LORD caused it?" (Amos 3:6). God says, "I bring prosperity and I create disaster." When times are good, God accepts responsibility; when times are bad and earthquakes erupt and hurricanes kill thousands of people, God still accepts responsibility. Who are we, as insignificant clay pieces, to decide what almighty God is powerless to do? Has God's masterpiece of creation spun chaotically out of control and ruined his sovereign plan? It doesn't tarnish God's holiness or love in the least to send a deadly hurricane upon a nation. Just look at the calamities God brought against the Canaanites, the Egyptians, and even his chosen nation of Israel in biblical times.

WHY DOESN'T GOD STOP EVIL?

A popular catchphrase in the church today is "It was a God thing." When our prayers for healing or safety are answered in a supernatural way, we label it "a God thing." When some good miraculously comes out of a murder or kidnapping, we term it "a God thing." But when something goes as horribly wrong as the rescue efforts following Hurricane Katrina, should we not also label even this "a God thing"?

When the "happy meals" of life arrive unexpectedly and supernaturally, it's "a God thing"; when our much-anticipated happy meals arrive

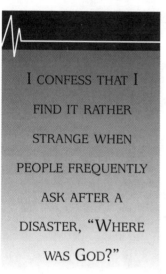

I CONFESS THAT I FIND IT RATHER STRANGE WHEN PEOPLE FREQUENTLY ASK AFTER A DISASTER, "WHERE WAS GOD?"

with no prize and the contents of the box looking like something in the dog's dish, it's just as much "a God thing." Truth be told, everything is a God thing. This is true even if humanity seems solely responsible for turning the box upside down and stomping on it—for we read in Proverbs 20:24, "A man's steps are directed by the LORD. How then can anyone understand his own way?" Psalm 33:10–11 tells us, "The LORD foils the plans of the nations; he thwarts the purposes of the peoples. But the plans of the LORD stand firm forever, the purposes of his heart through all generations."

Who knows how many years God held off a category four or five hurricane from striking New Orleans and the surrounding area? What's more surprising than the bumbled rescue efforts of FEMA is the fact that so many killer hurricanes over the decades have missed this part of the Gulf Coast. How many times was God publicly thanked in the '70s, '80s, '90s, and early years of this century for holding back a megahurricane the size of Katrina? Like the engineers, God knew for several years that the levees protecting New Orleans were not strong enough to protect the city from anything more than a category three hurricane. But few lend any thoughts to this now. Most just want to know, as on September 11, where God was when Katrina was killing hundreds of people and demolishing thousands of homes.

I confess that I find it rather strange when people frequently ask after a disaster, "Where was God?" Asking this question is like asking where a surgeon was when the patient's heart stopped beating on the operating room table. Where do you think the surgeon was? Sipping piña coladas while playing a round of golf at a nearby country club? *The surgeon was right by the patient's side.* It just *feels* as though he "left the room."

I've noticed something very interesting down through the years in the medical profession. I've never heard a medical doctor ask the question, "Where was God when this disaster struck?" Or, "How could a God of love allow this to happen?" Oh, I'm sure there are doctors who ask these very questions, but it seems very uncommon. Why? Because medical doctors understand better than most the fragility of life. There are a million and one ways to die in this world. If someone is going to trash talk God for allowing a handful of terrorists, or a megahurricane, to kill thousands of people, why not trash talk God for allowing an eighty-six-year-old woman to fall in the nursing home, break her hip, and a few days later die of a pulmonary embolism? Do you think God values one life over another (see Luke 12:6–7)? Do you think any one of the more than forty-five thousand people killed in the Pakistani earthquake a month after Katrina was any more or less loved by God?

Underneath these superficial dead skin cells we are all the same; we are all sinners; and, as medical doctors know, we are all dying. I overheard a radiologist telling a medical resident one day that death was inevitable. "Sooner or later one of your patients will die," he told the young doctor. "People die." Then he added with a chuckle, "Most people who are born do."

Now, you might think it rather odd that a specialist who spends most of his time in a dark room in front of flat monitors scrutinizing hundreds of digital images of live patients would be so accustomed to death. But radiologists see firsthand the "dying process" hundreds of times every week. Most X-rays of patients reveal some degenerative changes or disease(s)— evidence of the destructive death process underway in all our bodies. (It's not uncommon either for a patient to get an X-ray for right hip pain, only to have the radiologist see nothing abnormal in the right hip but find an ongoing degenerative disorder or an asymptomatic tumor in the left hip or pelvis.) The trillions of cells in our bodies are all programmed for death. Someone once said, "Health is merely the slowest possible rate at which one can die." We may feel perfectly healthy, but every one of us is dying on the inside. Radiologists, like any other medical specialists, understand well the brevity and ambiguity of life. This is just another reason why it is so irrational when people sporadically "blame" God every time a major tragedy erupts. Death is death; to question the existence, power, or love of God based on *how* someone dies is meaningless.

WHAT WE REALLY NEED IS MORE "SOUL-BUSTING" STRAIGHT TALK THAT BRINGS THE SINNER BACK TO REALITY.

Though God accepts responsibility for the aging process and for every calamity, he cannot be "blamed" in our usual way of thinking, as though we are the innocent paying tenants and he is the incompetent, uncaring landlord. We have signed no lease agreement with God to occupy his magnificent creation. We pay God no rent. No security deposit. No health insurance premiums. Nothing for utilities such as water, gas, and electricity. God has done a background credit check and found us all to be bankrupt (see Rom. 3:23). For some reason, however, he still allows us to live in his exclusive resort we call planet Earth. But when the gas is momentarily shut off, or our homes become flooded, or we fall sick with cancer, we attack God and demand that he fulfill his end of this nonexistent lease. Like Job, we even plead for our day in court to prove our innocence. Yet God's answer to us is the same as it was to Job: "Do you still want to argue with the Almighty? You are God's critic, but do you have the answers?" (Job 40:2 NLT).

With regard to Katrina, Dr. John MacArthur said this on his radio program:

> God does not consign himself to some necessity to answer
> our great questions.... This is a fallen world. You are sinful.

Calamity suits itself perfectly. It adapts perfectly to a fallen sinful world and a sinful humanity. It is inevitable. Death is inevitable. And you need to be prepared for it.[2]

Death is inevitable: That is God's message in these tragedies. It is also the same message Jesus Christ had for the people of his day. Wherever Christ traveled he preached that people were sinners. Death was certain for every individual. And eternal destruction in hell awaited those who refused to truly repent by turning away from their sin *to* Christ for salvation (see John 14:6; Matt. 25:41, 46). "Do not be afraid of those who kill the body but cannot kill the soul," warned Christ. "Rather, be afraid of the One who can destroy both soul and body in hell" (Matt. 10:28). He was continually warning his listeners that the judgment day was fast approaching. Christ preached death, judgment, and hell more often than televangelists beg for money today.

Today we have far too many "blockbuster preachers" whose main goal for their congregations is that they go home happy. There's little or no mention of God's wrath, his holiness, or his coming judgment. Sadly, the average person knows Homer Simpson better than he or she knows God; as a result, God's nature remains "a mystery wrapped inside a riddle inside an enigma."[3] And so the basic questions

May your unfailing love rest upon us, O Lord, even as we put our hope in you.

concerning God's nature just keep piling up in the minds of the ignorant. What we really need is less "blockbuster" motivational preaching and more "soul-busting" straight talk that brings the sinner back to reality. What's the point of going home happy if we will spend eternity in hell?

But was God sending the citizens of America a *second* message in Hurricane Katrina?

WHY DOESN'T GOD STOP EVIL?

Though we don't know the mind or purposes of God in this, there are some clear principles of which we can be reminded. In times of disaster it is so easy to put our trust in government, rather than in God. When a 145-mph hurricane roars toward a coastal community, Home Depot sells out of plywood and nails, and residents madly cram as many of their cherished possessions as possible into their vehicles and head for safer ground. It is just assumed that the government and local agencies will have emergency supplies on hand for those unable to escape the disaster zone. It is also assumed that immediate disaster relief will be available to clean up the mess afterward and rebuild a city.

But many citizens of the Gulf City had put their trust in the wrong person. God often uses good Samaritans to lend us a hand when we don't have the strength to lift up our own. But our trust needs to be in God—not mankind—for protection and salvation. Sometimes God rocks our world in an uncomfortable way so that we will take comfort, refuge, and hope in the one true Rock.

Psalm 33 might be God's personal message to the residents of New Orleans—as well as to the millions of Americans looking on.

> No king is saved by the size of his army; no warrior escapes by his great strength. A horse is a vain hope for deliverance; despite all its great strength it cannot save. But the eyes of the LORD are on those who fear him, on those whose hope is in his unfailing love, to deliver them from death and keep them alive in famine. We wait in hope for the LORD; he is our help and our shield. In him our hearts rejoice, for we trust in his holy name. May your unfailing love rest upon us, O LORD, even as we put our hope in you. (vv. 16–22)

What does the future hold? No one knows for sure except God. Likely more earthquakes, terrorist attacks, megahurricanes, wars, floods, famines, and killer viruses. I wish I could promise you that by next Monday the world will be a better place to live—but of course I can't. We simply live in a broken and sin-cursed world. What I do know for sure, however, is that the sovereign God of the universe is *my* Rock. "The Lord is my rock, my fortress and my deliverer;" proclaimed King

David (2 Sam. 22:2). God is also *my* hope, and *my* salvation. Why should I fear, knowing that my Creator is 100 percent in control of everything?

Though the events and details surrounding every subsequent disaster will change, I can say with complete confidence that I intimately know and understand the God I serve. And my God *never* changes. My hope and trust are in God—not mankind. Therefore, I will never be disappointed.

Whatever tomorrow holds, I know that my God holds it all in his hands. And in this my heart and soul rejoice!

WHY DOESN'T GOD STOP EVIL?

*That adult relationship reveals, I believe,
what God has always sought from human
beings: not the clinging, helpless love of a
child who has no real choice, but the
mature, freely given commitment of a lover.*[1]

—PHILIP YANCEY

7

THE TOUGHEST QUESTIONS ABOUT GOD

- If God is so powerful, why couldn't he have created a world without the possibility of evil?

- If God is all-powerful, why didn't he bind up or destroy the Devil right from the beginning?

- Why didn't God create us with more wisdom, so that we would always choose good over evil? And why doesn't he prove himself?

- If heaven is so great, why didn't God send us straight to paradise and forget earth all together?

- Why did God provide only one way of salvation? Doesn't this exclude millions of people in other religions?

Wise decisions are not always popular decisions. Just ask any veteran politician who has tried to close down an inefficient hospital in an effort to save money and consolidate services, staff time, and state-of-the-art equipment for overall improvement in a city's healthcare plan. He or she will be lucky to escape the ordeal without a death threat!

WHY DOESN'T GOD STOP EVIL?

Often criticism is leveled at God when we cannot see the beautiful mosaic through God's wide lens. "Like a deaf critic of Bach or a blind critic of Raphael is the unregenerate [unbelieving] critic of God's Word."[2] It is impossible for an unbeliever under the bondage of sin to see life through God's eyes. Consequently, God's wise decisions are usually not the most popular decisions with most of the world's population.

In reading through a publication from the American Humanist Association, *The Humanist*, I encountered many tough questions raised about God by an unbeliever.[3] I've already tackled, in previous chapters and in another book in this series,[††] some of these questions, but I thought it might be worthwhile to deal with some of the toughest questions here, along with other questions later. If you are a mature believer, these "hurdles" will not pose a significant threat to your faith; you may already have a decent handle on the "secret things" about God; but rest assured, if your Christian life is a shining light, someone will inevitably take notice and try to extinguish it by challenging you to come up with some answers for these tough questions.

I don't, admittedly, have all the solutions to these problems posed about God. These are really tough questions. But hopefully, by taking a closer look through the pages of Scripture into the issues fueling these questions, we'll be able to better rearrange our stepping-stones, and in the end, have some answer for those who question our faith.

Q: If God is so powerful, why couldn't he have created a world without the possibility of evil?

No question has so firmly anchored the agnostic and atheist in the bewitching sea of disbelief than the plaguing question, "Where did evil come from?" If God exists, and if he is so good, so wise, and so powerful, why didn't he create us without the option of sinning? Why were our natures vulnerable to "cracking"?

Good questions. You'll remember from previous chapters that evil originated from within Adam, Eve, and Satan when they sinned. Evil is

---

†† *Is God Obsolete?*

not a substance, as St. Augustine rightly argues. It is the absence of and distorted arrangement of good. A perfectly functioning watch will display the wrong time if you remove or rearrange any of its perfect parts. "Evil" can be thought of as something good that has become broken or defective. We have huge cracks in the core of our beings; we can see the effects of evil caused from these cracks, albeit, there is no real substance of evil there. (There is nothing in a "crack.") Therefore evil is not of God, in God, or created by God.

Now, we could struggle through pages and pages of philosophic arguments over the existence of God and evil, but let's move right to the crux of this debate. The primary reason this hurdle looms as large as it does in our minds is because of mankind's imagination. The human race imagines two things:

1. A creature could be created with a meaningful free will without the possibility of doing evil.
2. This good world, devoid of evil, would be better for us and God than a world tainted with evil.

Now, few would consciously argue that our imaginations and reasonings are 100 percent perfect; but unconsciously, this is the mistake many have made. In holding to such a line of subliminal thinking, the imagination of the clay is automatically deemed superior to the wisdom and intellect of the Potter. Stop and think about that for a moment. How absurd is it to denounce the existence or power of God because the clay cannot imagine how the Potter could ultimately use evil for his greatest glory?

Right here, humanity is irrationally implying that we know the mind of God—that we top our transcendent Creator in the intelligence department (if this Creator even exists, some may argue). And because humanity can't wrap our neurons around the baffling problem of evil, to figure out how evil could be used for God's greatest glory, then we can't accept the existence of an all-powerful God.

Paul would immediately denounce such outlandish "imaginings": "No one knows the thoughts of God except the Spirit of God," declared the apostle (1 Cor. 2:11b). Dr. John MacArthur states: "Man is as far from comprehending the infinite mind of God, as clay is from comprehending the mind of the Potter."[4] Humanity has no hope of intellectually fathoming the full extent of God's priorities and his ways. What hope do we have of understanding God's infinite mind?

In broaching the question, "Why couldn't God have created a world without evil?" the distinguished Catholic philosopher and professor, Peter Kreeft, argues, "Creating a world where there's free will and no possibility of sin is a self-contradiction."[5]

C. S. Lewis says:

> Some people think they can imagine a creature which was free but had no possibility of going wrong; I cannot. If a thing is free to be good it is also free to be bad. And free will is what has made evil possible.[6]

Geisler and Feinberg wonder:

> Would a world where sin was never permitted be the *best* world or only a good one? ... Is it not better to permit some evil for achieving the greater good? Certain levels of virtue and pleasure cannot be attained without permitting some pain and evil. It may be that God permitted this evil world as a means of producing the greatest good.[7]

The two authors maintain that we have "good evidence" for believing that we live in "the best world achievable within the limits of freedom and dignity." God's "own infinitely good nature is all the reason one could ever need."[8]

Why is our perceived free will so important to God? Ask yourself, "Would God receive the glory he does now if we had the free will of a robot?" Gerard Reed writes, "One of the glowing vestiges of God's image still evident in man, shining like a house light on a darkened porch, is his free will."[9] How do we know that God would receive more glory if this "darkened porch" never existed? Would our free will bring the maximum amount of glory to God if it were unable to "shine forth" against the backdrop of a world darkened by evil?

THE TOUGHEST QUESTIONS ABOUT GOD

One cannot rule out the supremacy of God simply because evil exists unless one knows the mind of God—to know what would please God the most. To imagine that we could have created a better world than God is as foolish and futile as a stone imagining it could run for secretary-general of the United Nations.

Why has God allowed evil? I have to confess that this "free will" answer above doesn't get us very far across the raging river of evil. In fact, if you study Scripture closely, you will find that this answer leaves us with one foot still stuck in the mud on the riverbank. Do we really have a so-called free will that is not influenced or controlled by God in any way? A slew of Scripture verses would say we don't, including Proverbs 20:24; 21:1; Ezekiel 36:22–32; Daniel 4:35; John 6:37, 44, 65; Romans 9:14–21; and Ephesians 1:4–12.

Actually, the real answer for why evil exists is tucked away in a passage of Scripture that is almost completely ignored by the leaders in most churches because it is seen as too "offensive"—to unbelievers and believers. But how can we ever hope to understand the rich character of God if we purposely ignore the answers in his Word, simply because we don't like them?

You might remember the true story of how God led the children of Israel out of Egypt, and how he molded the lives of Moses and Pharaoh for his greatest glory. The apostle Paul writes:

> For the Scripture says to Pharaoh: "I raised you up for this very purpose, that I might display my power in you and that my name might be proclaimed in all the earth." Therefore God has mercy on whom he wants to have mercy, and he hardens whom he wants to harden." (Rom. 9:17–18)

A few verses further on, Paul explains a little more why God might create some people for noble purposes and others to display his wrath and justice.

> Does not the potter have the right to make out of the same lump of clay some pottery for noble purposes and some for

common use? What if God, choosing to show his wrath and make his power known, bore with great patience the objects of his wrath—prepared for destruction? What if he did this to make the riches of his glory known to the objects of his mercy, whom he prepared in advance for glory—even us, whom he also called, not only from the Jews but also from the Gentiles? (Rom. 9:21–24)

Paul tells us that evil exists so that God might "show his wrath and make his power known" (Rom. 9:22; see also 9:18; 11:32). "Surely your wrath against men brings you praise," writes the psalmist (Ps. 76:10a). That's a pretty tough dose of reality medicine, isn't it? Does evil exist primarily so that God might have an opportunity to display to the greatest degree all of his marvelous perfections—including his mercy, his love, and his justice? If evil had never existed, we, "the objects of his mercy," would *never* have come to appreciate God's justice, wrath, power, patience, mercy, and grace. We would be worshipping a God who, for all we knew, was a single-dimensional God of goodness. God's true glory would have gone unrecognized for all of eternity. To purposely conceal the greatness of his character forever would have been character assassination for God. (That doesn't mean, though, that we should be buying up real estate in "Sin City" in an attempt to promote God's agenda of grace [see Rom. 6:1–4].)

In tackling this question head on in a mature manner, we catch a glimpse of God's real purpose in his divine parenting strategies through history. God's primary objective was not to "parent" the world for the sake of parenting alone, to have someone to love and converse with, but to richly manifest each perfection of his majestic character at different stages of history. Take a good look into yourself. When is each facet of your multidimensional character set high on a pedestal for all to see? Answer: when you're a parent—whether you like it not. For this is when your wisdom, creativity, ingenuity, justice, power, discipline, love, patience, mercy, and kindness are all modeled completely naked before your children and for everyone else to see.

Remember the earlier story of the medical doctor who left America to treat the Nigerian AIDS patients? He only had enough medication ("magic seeds") left to treat five patients for one year, yet he gave all the medication to the witch doctor who cursed his name. Why? Because the medical doctor's *primary* objective was not to make as many people as possible happy and healthy, but to demonstrate his generosity and grace. By giving five times as much medication to the evil witch doctor, who seemed to deserve it the least, the American doctor displayed his generosity and grace to a much greater degree.

Similarly with God: His *primary* objective is not to pull a "blockbuster" to make everyone go home happy; his *primary* aim is not to make every saint healthy to live another year; rather, it is to display his perfections to the maximum glory *to himself.* By giving just as much—or more—of his "magic seeds" of grace to the wicked, to let them live another day, God is displaying much more of his generosity, mercy, and grace than if he made a hundred times as many loyal saints happy and healthy. God may be concerned with our happiness, but he is obsessed with his glory.

There is one big difference, however. The medical doctor was lacking in the self-esteem department. His medical colleagues and patients had criticized him for not being generous enough, which is why he set out to prove to himself that they were wrong. That's why he gave the evil witch doctor all that medication. In contrast, God has no legitimate "need" to display his glory in and through his creation. God, unlike the medical doctor, is not lacking in the self-esteem category— or in any other category for that matter. We can say that evil exists to show off God's glory, but when we come to the tougher question— "What is the reason God 'needs' to promote his glory?"—perhaps the only answer we can come up with is, "because he can." God *is* God; it's who he is. All this may not fit with the god you've created in your mind, but it fits with the God revealed throughout the pages of his number one best-selling book of all time.

As a Bible teacher once said, God is the hero of history, using cycles of judgment and restoration to raise his children, thereby revealing to the greatest extent his glorious person. What's quite interesting, however, as we look back through history, is that God doesn't seem to care that believers in each generation at a specific time appreciate every one of his perfections.

WHY DOESN'T GOD STOP EVIL?

For example, the Israelites experienced firsthand the awesome power of God when he held back the Red Sea to allow a couple of million Jews to cross on dry ground. The tiny nation came to better appreciate the holiness, justice, and righteousness of God when their Lord gave them the Ten Commandments, along with a number of strict formal procedures and laws that surrounded building, maintaining, and worshipping in the tabernacle. The following generation would grasp even better the Almighty's wrath and justice when God brought down the mighty walls of Jericho and righteously judged the wicked Canaanite nations. Those who walked the earth with Christ came to experience in a marvelous way the compassion and love of God through Christ's actions. Believers in the early church came away with a marvelous appreciation of God's grace and mercy when they came through the transition period from the Mosaic Law to the law of grace.

What about more recent times? In the past few centuries, believers have come to develop a healthier fear of the Lord through a better understanding of the *holiness* and *majesty* of God—more specifically his greatness and splendor. While the children of Israel possessed a fear that leaned more toward an irrational dread, those living in the past half millennium seem to have a healthier fear of God. This has trickled down through the years to the older generation living today. The oldest generation in evangelical churches tends to have a special reverence for God, viewing him as the royal King of heaven who demands our utmost respect. They see him in their minds as a majestic ruler, seated on his rightful throne in heaven, running the affairs of the world, directing people by opening and closing doors—trying his best to keep believers in his individual will for their lives. God seemingly must abide by some intrinsic law of fairness that allows people to stray in their free will and mess up his agenda from time to time.

This thinking is undergoing some serious changes, however. The younger generations, in contrast, tend to view God as a "good buddy" who is right down in the trenches of life with all of us, with his hands in anything and everything. Generation X and Generation D (D for digital) understand better than probably any other generation in history that God is in complete control of everything; that if he wants to do something, he just does it. God is absolutely free from all controlling influences, which means the human race and the Devil cannot mess up his prearranged plans. And if God, the Potter, wants to create some clay vessels as "objects of his wrath," as Romans so clearly states, then so be it. God holds that unrestricted right as our Creator. Consequently, the younger generation is not nearly as concerned with trying to stay within some mysterious "individual will" for our lives—because no matter what happens, God's plan will be done, and God will lead them wherever he wants.

These differences between the generations are visible in the songs we sing—and the T-shirts we wear (or might not wear). A quick search on the Internet produces dozens of sites selling Christian T-shirts, targeted mainly at Generation D, with slogans such as these:

> Jesus is WHASSUP in my life!
> Jesus would have been a biker
> Hang loose with Jesus

But the T-shirt that I think best demonstrates the attitude in Generations D and X features the commonly seen caricature of a rolypoly character in four positions splitting his side laughing just above the caption, "God can't do what?"

The older generation tends to picture God as the supreme and revered ruler in heaven, the "King of kings" and "Lord of lords," while the younger generations tend to picture God as "a friend who sticks closer than a brother"—someone who is right beside them laughing just as hard on the floor with the reply, "God can't do what?" We are not perfect, and we often mess up and sin, but somehow everything works out according to what God wants, because he is absolutely sovereign and does whatever he wishes.

While the older generation of believers today tends to have a healthier fear of God, resulting from a better understanding of one aspect of God's *majesty*, the younger generation tends to have a better understanding of God's *sovereignty*. Neither view of God is necessarily better than the other. Both miss the mark in some way when it comes to a true understanding of God.

WHY DOESN'T GOD STOP EVIL?

However, I believe we are living in a very special time in history. A young generation of believers, bucking certain myths created by the church over the centuries, has broken free to arrive at a better appreciation of the sovereignty of God.[10]

God even goes as far as to shape the culture of a particular era to help the people of the day better appreciate and understand his "attribute of the century." For example, in our culture we enjoy many freedoms in the realm of travel, education, sports, and the arts. We have so many choices when it comes to vacations, computer hardware, software, fast-food menus, clothes, cell phones, cars, and thousands of accessories, that we can pretty much pick and choose exactly what we want to custom fit our desires—without even leaving the comfort of our home and our Internet browser. So, if we have this right and privilege to pick and choose what we want—to organize our lives how we want to live—then why shouldn't God our Creator do that for his highest delight? Consequently, it sure isn't a very big leap off the old logic bridge with the bungee cord of common sense wrapped tight around our ankles to believe that God, our Creator, "does as he pleases with the powers of heaven and the peoples of the earth. No one can hold back his hand or say to him: 'What have you done?'" (Dan. 4:35b).

Consequently, most generations of believers throughout history have had the divine privilege to witness firsthand, and truly appreciate, at least one mighty perfection of God. When you understand this fact, Bible history will make so much more sense to you. You'll find yourself rearranging your stepping-stones so quickly it will take you days or weeks to finish the task and get your mind to stop spinning. In contrast, those who argue that God *must* act the same way today as he did hundreds or thousands of years ago have little understanding of God's divine character and his purpose.[11] Their stepping-stones remain haphazardly scattered along the riverbank. As a result, they have little hope of getting even halfway across the raging river of evil.

No generation of believers in history, as a whole, has had a perfectly well-rounded understanding of all of God's perfections. But then again, our eternal God doesn't seem to care. This tells us something very, very important about our Creator. Who really needs to be impressed by the matchless power, justice, righteousness, love, grace, mercy, holiness, majesty, and sovereignty of almighty God?

God.

Our stepping-stones begin to fit nicely into place across the raging river of evil when we understand that only God needs to be truly impressed by his glory.

A world without evil would have been a good world all right, but it would not have been the best world from God's perspective.

THE ETERNITY OF GOD: ANOTHER CLUE

An additional reason that many believe that God cannot coexist with evil is that evil is said to introduce injustice into the world. The Bible reveals justice to be a core value of God, so many believe that he could never exist in a universe contaminated with the horridness of evil. How can he let the murderer or rapist get away with the evil such a person inflicts on mankind? Christians counter with the statement that one day God will thwart the "powers of evil" and fully restore justice.

In Martin Luther King Jr.'s famous 1963 "I Have a Dream" speech, he proclaimed, "We will not be satisfied until justice rolls down like waters and righteousness like a mighty stream."[12] Is God completely satisfied if this justice doesn't "roll down" right away? Many Christians contend that God won't be satisfied until perfect justice is accomplished. God, the average believer argues, is still working on the final "mosaic" to bring the most glory to him.

But remember that our God is an eternal, transcendent God. God exists in the past, present, and future "simultaneously." God exists as an eternal being, existing everywhere along and outside our time line. From God's perspective, he is living and working in every point in time—in the eternal *now*. He is not like us, handcuffed by the restraints of time.

If you can get some grasp of this difficult concept, you'll understand then that there really is no such thing as "injustice" as seen through God's "wide lens" (see Rom. 3:5–6; 9:14). For God exists in a time when justice is being served. When six million Jews were slaughtered in the Holocaust, God's anger erupted like a corked volcano and his heart was sickened. But from God's perspective through his "wide lens," perfect justice was already satisfied. The unbelievers committing the heinous acts of genocide were already serving their just recompense in hell.

Therefore, the injustice that we see from our perspective is not a problem for God because the Almighty exists concurrently in a time when evil has been fully conquered and justice restored.[13] If Christ did not die on the cross to pay the penalty for our sins, there would be injustice if God took sinners to heaven. And if hell did not exist, then all those who rejected Christ would go scot-free. Therefore, from God's perspective, injustice would exist only if Christ had not died on the cross and if hell did not exist. Evil, then, does nothing to tarnish God's justice. (Maybe this is one reason Christ didn't run around the earth debating and agonizing over the existence of evil.)

Comprehending a little more how God exists inside *and* outside the dimension of time radically changes our way of thinking. It sheds a much different light on how the Almighty views evil. And the pieces in our minds fall into place. For example, we read in Genesis 15:6, "Abram believed the LORD, and he credited it to him as righteousness." How could Abraham and his children who would have faith in God be justified by faith in God's sight and receive imputed righteousness *before* Christ's death (see Rom. 4:9, 13)? If it is only by the shed blood of Christ that we have true forgiveness of sins and eternal salvation, how was Abraham viewed by God "just as if" he had never sinned?

The likely answer is that God exists everywhere in time—in the beginning, middle, and end of time simultaneously. When Abraham was walking the earth, our Creator concurrently existed in time when Christ's blood was being shed on the cross. Through God's "wide lens," Christ, the perfect sacrifice, had already shed his blood on the cross for Abraham's sins. Therefore, there was no "injustice" from God's point of view in pardoning and imputing righteousness to Abraham. God was able to see Abraham as perfect through the death of his Son thousands of years later in his "wide lens," even though God was fully aware of Abraham's ancient-day sins at the moment as seen through the Divine's "narrow lens."

While evil might be a problem for us, it is certainly not a problem for God. Evil to God is just another mosaic piece that he uses in building the most beautiful mosaic possible. God uses the good, the bad, and the ugly for his greatest glory (see Rom. 8:28).

Yet we harbor a second misconception: We believe that God won't get to see this beautiful mosaic and be fully satisfied until evil is finally conquered. Christendom clings to the delusion that God, after watching sin enter his perfect world, set in motion "plan B" to get everything back to the point where he will once again be satisfied with a perfect universe.

Is this view of God correct? What if everything *right now* is exactly the way God wants it to be? What if every single event and action *right now* is what God planned as part of his permissive and directive will an eternity ago (see Dan. 4:35)? Despite the multitude of Bible verses I've quoted and referenced so far in this book extolling the absolute sovereignty of God, some would still label me a heretic for even suggesting such a thing.

Remember, though, that God exists everywhere along *and outside of* our time line. Therefore, this perfect, exquisitely beautiful mosaic, bringing maximum glory and delight to him, has been front and center of God's "wide lens" since eternity past. Many would prefer to think in terms of God still adding the "pieces of evil" to his mosaic, but in reality, God had completely designed this mosaic before he even created Adam and Eve. From God's perspective, the mosaic is complete and incredibly lovely. No other design could have been any better. God's *one and only* plan for the universe, from his perspective, is already accomplished. *There is never a "plan B" with God.*

Since evil fits perfectly into God's perfect agenda, to totally eliminate the possibility of evil would have been, for God, like taking a sledgehammer the size of a galaxy to his precious mosaic—smashing it into a million jagged pieces. To us, allowing evil is senseless; to God, it is crucial to his plan—something that we cannot fully comprehend with our finite minds.

We will return again to the question of evil, in this and other books in the series, to see more precisely how it fits into God's perfectly designed blueprint.

Q: If God is all-powerful, why didn't he bind up or destroy the Devil right from the beginning?

Though this book focuses on understanding God better, this question requires that we also understand something about the Devil. Seventeenth-century Puritan Stephen Charnock pointed out some personal qualities about the Prince of Demons that you might not have thought about.

1. The Devil possesses more of God's natural goodness than we do: All living creatures, be they animals, humans, angels, or demons, possess at least some degree of their Creator's natural goodness. The Devil possesses more "natural goodness" than we do because he has "more marks of the excellency of God upon him...." What Charnock means is that the Devil is more like God than we are in that he is an invisible spirit who is more powerful, knowledgeable, and wiser (in an earthly sense) than we.[14]

2. "The Devil is not more fallen from the rectitude [goodness] of his nature and likeness to God than we are": Humanity possesses the potential to carry out evil on a scale equal to that of the Devil—except for two reasons: a) mankind is less powerful than the Devil and b) God may be restraining evil in mankind more than he does the Devil.[15] (See Eph. 4:18–19.)

Chaining up Satan to curb evil would have demonstrated God's goodness.[16] But by keeping Satan free, relatively speaking, Satan's evil ways become like those of a rebellious child, set loose to smash glass, unknowingly, in a glass-smashing factory. The child thinks he is destroying good glass, when in truth, he is only helping to break up the glass into valuable pieces that can be constructively used, for example, as filler in the road-paving process. (Yes, they actually use glass for this purpose.)

Satan, like this rebellious child, thinks he is destroying good glass, when in fact, he is only breaking up the pieces to perfectly fit into God's beautiful mosaic to make it "sparkle." To Satan and us, these pieces look ugly and senseless; but only God knows just how valuable these pieces really are.

Several examples from Scripture demonstrate this truth. God removed his "holy fire" from Pharaoh's heart (took away his restraining presence) to allow it to harden on its own (see also Prov. 21:1). Consequently, Pharaoh did exactly what he wanted to do in his depraved state of sinfulness. Very likely the Devil was also allowed a firm grip on the ruler's heart—preventing the children of Israel from leaving Egypt. But through Satan's and Pharaoh's evil actions God accomplished good:

1. Justice was brought upon the idolatrous Egyptians for their sins against God and the Israelites.

2. The Egyptians wanted the Israelites out so bad, they gave them exorbitant amounts of gold, silver, wood, and expensive cloth (their past wages) that would be later used in the building of the Lord's temple.

3. God used the harsh treatment by the Egyptians as a catalyst to move the Israelites out of Egypt and into the Promised Land.

4. Each plague was allowed by God to attack the specific parallel "god" of Egypt (i.e., the hail undermined the power of "Nut," the sky goddess, and "Set," the god of storms). By doing so, God demonstrated His incontestable supremacy to the Egyptians, Israelites, and every surrounding nation.[17]

WHY DOESN'T GOD STOP EVIL?

It's interesting that most accounts of highly visible demon possession occurred for only a brief period around the time of Christ. No doubt God allowed demons to possess the people in order that his divine purposes would be accomplished. The demons indirectly helped to spread the gospel in two ways:

1. Some people turned to God out of fear of these violent spirits. In our era, *The Exorcist* ranks as one of the scariest movies of all time.

2. Casting out the demons authenticated the powers of Christ and the apostles, thereby authenticating and heralding their gospel message. One major reason that highly visible cases of demon possession are rarely seen today is that the demons learned their lesson two thousand years ago. For the Devil to remind people that there is a cosmic spiritual battle underway is to shoot himself in the foot.

God also restrains the Devil and his demons much more than the average believer thinks. In the book of Job, we learn that, though Satan is a very powerful enemy, God keeps him on a very short leash. Satan is accountable to God for his whereabouts and must seek permission from God every single time before harming those God protects (see Job 1). Perhaps this world wouldn't be drastically different if the Devil didn't exist. Humankind is perfectly capable of carrying out the most wicked deeds imaginable without any help.

Anyone can orchestrate good out of good; the Devil is clever at orchestrating evil out of good. But only God can orchestrate *good out of evil* (see Rom. 8:28). For God to use Satan's fiendish ways to bring about his divine glorious and gracious ends, not only further demonstrates God's goodness, says Charnock, but it also manifests his unsurpassed power and wisdom.[18] The Devil, unknowingly, is actually helping God to win the "Coach of the Year" award and build the most stunning mosaic possible.

Since God receives more glory by allowing the Devil limited reign, to completely chain up or destroy the Devil would have been a very unwise decision on God's part.

Q: Why didn't God create us with more wisdom so that we would always choose good over evil? And why doesn't he prove himself?

Does being sufficiently wise automatically imply that we will choose good over evil every time?

I would argue it doesn't.

The Lord said concerning Satan: "'You were the model of perfection, full of wisdom and perfect in beauty'" (Ezek. 28:12b). One of the most knowledgeable and wisest creatures ever created was the Devil—yet he still rebelled against God. Adam, in his perfect state, was told the consequences of disobeying God—yet he still took a bite of the fruit. Solomon, saturated with wisdom, let his heart be led astray into idol worship by his pagan wives. All these individuals had "sufficient wisdom" to choose good—yet they still chose evil.

Why? Because even when we know there will be repercussions from our sinful actions, the tempting, temporal pleasures of life often win out. In a sense, Adam, Solomon, and the Devil all made wise decisions within themselves, based on their own "values." They weighed the imagined consequences against the perceived benefits, and still chose evil because that's what they really wanted.

You see, our problem isn't so much a lack of wisdom as it is a *lack of holiness*. Wisdom without holiness is like a building without a foundation. Without a wholesome base to our decision-making process, our "moral choices" crumble.

You might respond, "Well, why didn't God just create us with his perfect holiness and infinite knowledge—guaranteeing that we'd always make the right decisions? Instead of basing our decisions on our 'values,' why didn't God create us so that we would always make decisions based on *his* values?"

We've already discovered how evil fits perfectly into God's plan to display every one of his glorious perfections. But could God have created us with his degree of holiness and omniscience? Could God create another God? There's only room for one God inside and outside this universe, so I would have to answer no to this highly abstract question (see Isa. 42:8; 48:11).

What about creating us with more knowledge? Often we make unwise decisions because we don't know the future.

I remember, as a youngster, watching a *Gilligan's Island* episode in which the seven stranded castaways discovered some magic berries that, when eaten, allowed them to read each others' minds. At first it was an entertaining novelty that eliminated the need for chitchat. After a while, though, they turned on each other like vicious bulls. As hateful, and malicious thoughts popped into their minds, they became more and more angry at one another. In the end, Gilligan destroyed the berry bushes, restoring peace and love on the island.

Imagine how much more evil and hate would exist on this planet if we had more knowledge. If we could more accurately predict the weather, stock markets, and sports games, if we could solve all the mysteries of astronomy, medicine, and physics, if we could, to some degree, read people's minds, think of the torrent of pride, deceit, greed, and maliciousness this would unleash on the world. Every time we human beings think we know everything, we turn our back on God.

Besides, absolute proof or knowledge of God's existence probably wouldn't make that much difference anyway. The angels know full well that our all-powerful God exists, yet millions, perhaps as many as one third of all angels fell, or will fall, as demons (see Rev. 12:4). The influential German philosopher Friedrich Nietzsche likely echoed the thoughts of many atheists and agnostics when he said, "If you could prove God to me, I would believe Him all the less."[19] Recall also that God appeared to Israel in many forms, but they frequently lost faith in Jehovah.

Best-selling Christian author Lee Strobel tells the story of how, when he was an atheist, the doctors were unable to diagnose his newborn daughter's life-threatening illness. Desperate for help, Strobel cried out to God (unsure if he existed) to miraculously heal his little girl. And God did in an astonishing way—leaving the doctors "scratching their heads."

What did Strobel do? Did he automatically put his faith in God? Strobel's response was, "'What a coincidence! She must have had some bacteria or virus that spontaneously disappeared.' I wouldn't even consider the possibility that God had acted. Instead, I stayed in my atheism."[20] For Strobel, his spiritual struggle was not with an imaginary God he could not see, but rather, with a "visible" God he did not want.[21]

Even if God were to write his name across the sky, appear on national television, or stand on everyone's living room floor, likely one third or more of the world would refuse to worship him. And the majority of the other two-thirds would bow to their heavenly Father only out of duty—not out of hearts of love and reverence.

Q: If heaven is so great, why didn't God send us straight to paradise and forget Earth all together?

Some famous Christian authors say we were "created for heaven." Those who believe such, however, have a heap of trouble answering this tough question.

Part of the answer rides on the coat tails of the previous responses. God has his reasons for withholding some knowledge from us—especially absolute, conclusive proof of his existence. A believer's genuine, childlike faith, stemming from a reverent and obedient heart, ranks extremely high on God's priority list. Worshipping a proven supreme being simply because you feel it is your celestial duty just wouldn't cut it with God. God's glory and the genuine faith of a believer rank number one and number two on God's all-time priority list.

One reason God didn't send us straight to heaven is because our worship, based solely on faith, is enormously valuable to God. By placing us on this earth, God has given us the opportunity to choose him—not out of fear or obligation—but out of love.[22] Worshipping God out of obligation would be like loving your spouse because it was your duty—or because someone was paying you to do so. "Hey, honey? Did our marriage contract state I was to say 'I love you' every Saturday—or every Sunday evening?"

WHY DOESN'T GOD STOP EVIL?

We know sin does not exist in heaven. How God accomplishes this we don't exactly know. If he decides to limit our free will so that we can't sin, our worship will still be meaningful to God because we worshipped God and chose him in faith here on earth. "Without faith it is impossible to please God," we read in Hebrews 11:6. This meaningful worship wouldn't have existed had God sent us straight to heaven. When we stand in paradise, singing out our joyous acclamations to God, at the forefront of his mind will be the fact that we bowed the knee to him out of love—not obligation (see 1 John 4:19).

There's a second reason why God didn't drop us off prematurely at the pearly gates. By creating mankind on earth and sending Christ to redeem us, we have a "more excellent condition than Adam had in innocence."[23] What Charnock means by this is that Adam, in his innocent state, had holiness that could be lost. In Christ we will be perfect—we will have holiness conferred on us that can never be lost throughout all of eternity (see Rom. 4:16; 8:38–39).[24]

Therefore, we were not "created for heaven." God did not place us here on earth because he had no other way of training us for heaven. It is quite clear in Scripture that individuals like Pharaoh were *never* created for heaven (see Rom. 9:14–24). When you understand all the good that can come out of evil, good that would never have been possible had God sent us straight to heaven, you will understand that we were created primarily for earth *right now.* Heaven is just one part of God's perfect plan for the universe. By itself, it is not *the* ultimate plan from God's view.

Bypassing earth and sending the human race straight to heaven would have been as meaningless for God as proving himself and creating us without the potential for sin.[25]

Q: Does God provide only one way of salvation? If so, doesn't this exclude millions of people in other religions?

Religious experts such as Harold Kushner, author of *Who Needs God*, maintains, "Religions can disagree and still each be true."[26]

Every major religion in the world, apart from Christianity, believes that Jesus Christ *was not* the Son of God. But to a genuine Christian, the very heart of our faith is grounded in Christ's deity. Saying that all religions can be true is like saying that Christ is the Son of God and that he isn't the Son of God.

"What difference does it make?" some still ask. It makes all the difference in the world! If Christ is not the Son of God, then Christianity splinters apart into the butt of all jokes. But if Christ is God's only begotten Son, as we read throughout the New Testament, then this has far-reaching implications for those who insist that every path leads to God. For Christ said, "I am *the* way and *the* truth and *the* life. No one comes to the Father *except* through me" (John 14:6).

Further on, Kushner clarifies his argument: "Religious claims can be true at a level other than the factual one." He maintains that truth centers subjectively on who one is as a spiritual being. Since "people's spiritual needs come in different forms," says the author, some of us require different religions.[27]

But Kushner is forgetting one very important detail: truth is not centered around who we are, or on what we need. "Truth is as old as God," writes Emily Dickinson.[28] Reading through the Scriptures, it becomes readily apparent that God has only *one* way of doing things: *his way.*

As much as we may fight God's nature and wisdom, our Creator *is* truth—not us. God's perfect plan of redemption was never introduced to satisfy our individual needs—it was introduced to satisfy God's justice.

Reconsider the illustration of the eight-year-old child who is dying of a rare disease. Imagine if the child were to give the world-renowned medical doctor the hand: "Don't want to hear it, Doc. You can take your drugs and shove them up …"

How foolish of the clay to balk at the Potter's life-saving gift of salvation just because the soggy-headed piece of mud believes there is a better lifeline to eternal life. How can anyone criticize the Lord of lords for offering a perfect gift to all of us as sinners when we are completely undeserving of his grace and mercy? Voting to change God's perfect spiritual law of redemption is as insane as voting to change God's physical law of gravity.[29] It's carved in stone, and the majority never rules.

The *one* true God who never changes in his nature created *one* universe. He chose *one* nation, Israel, to influence *one* world. He gave them *one* law. He inspired *one* Bible with *one* gospel for *one* planet. In his *one* and only sovereign plan, he sent his *one* Son down to *one* earth to live *once*, die *once*, be resurrected *once*, and to pay the penalty for our sins *once*. Why is it so hard to accept that God would have only *one* way to him? If every path leads to God, and Christ didn't need to die for our sins, why then did God needlessly send his only Son to earth to be grotesquely crucified by humankind? Wouldn't this make God the most sadistic being that ever lived?

The reason so many find God's one way of salvation hard to accept is that it seems to exclude so many "moral" people. (The word *sinner* is extremely offensive to a nonbeliever.) Yet in God's eyes, not one of us is moral. The hidden sins of the heart—those deep, ugly cracks—keep all of us separated from our most holy God.

How are we saved? Paul explains everything in simple terms. "That if you confess with your mouth, 'Jesus is Lord,' and believe in your heart that God raised him from the dead, you will be saved" (Rom. 10:9). Salvation demands genuine repentance and faith; God has made the gospel so clear that even a seven-year-old can understand it.

Listen to the words in Scripture:

> We are made right in God's sight when we trust in Jesus Christ to take away our sins. And we all can be saved in this same way, no matter who we are or what we have done. For all have sinned; all fall short of God's glorious standard. Yet now God in his gracious kindness declares us not guilty. He has done this through Christ Jesus, who has freed us by taking away our sins. For God sent Jesus to take the punishment for our sins and to satisfy God's anger against us. We are made right with God when we believe that Jesus shed his blood, sacrificing his life for us.... Can we boast, then, that we have done anything to be accepted by God? No, because our acquittal is not based on our

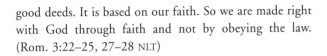

good deeds. It is based on our faith. So we are made right with God through faith and not by obeying the law. (Rom. 3:22–25, 27–28 NLT)

It is only through the shed blood of Jesus Christ, the only perfect, divine person to ever walk the earth, that our heavenly Father accepts us. All God asks is that we put our faith in him by repenting and submitting. You'd be hard-pressed to convince your spouse that sleeping with someone else is "submitting" to the marriage relationship. In like manner, you'd be hard-pressed to convince our heavenly Father that ritualistically worshipping other gods, prophets, "energy forces," or yourself is true submission to him.

But is God's plan of salvation really as exclusionary as some people think? Ted Koppel made this statement on national television:

> It is hard to envision such a God condemning hundreds of millions of people simply because they lacked the foresight to be born into the religion that we happen to believe in or because, in later years, they remain faithful to the religion of their birth.[30]

Two truths need to be clarified here: *First*, eternal salvation does not hinge on the particular religion you're born into. I always dislike using the term *Christianity* together with the term *religion* because so many people believe God accepts them for just being biologically born into a "Christian" family. God doesn't care if you're born into a Christian, Muslim, Hindu, or Buddhist family. It makes absolutely no difference to God at all. God never condemns us for being born into the "wrong religion."

> Then Peter began to speak: "I now realize how true it is that God does not show favoritism but accepts men from every nation who fear him and do what is right." (Acts 10:34–35)

Second, everyone is offered God's free gift of salvation, no matter what religion one is born into (see John 3:16). The choice we have is to yield to God or ignore him. Have you ever met a teenager who blindly followed the family religion without revolting or questioning the beliefs at least once? Who hasn't asked, "Why am I doing this?" To argue that Hindus, Muslims, and Buddhists blindly practice the religion they do strictly because of their birthplace or birth family is an insult to these people. It reduces these intelligent individuals to the status of mindless robots who cannot think or act for themselves.

I've come to notice over the years that those who criticize God's Scripture-based plan of salvation the most are usually the ones who submit to a belief system the least. Atheists, agnostics, and New Agers believe that even if God exists, it doesn't matter—they're safe because of their "morals." They presume that if a personal God is indeed real, then every "moral" path must lead to him. (Such individuals are blinded by the common denominator—an ill-defined moral system that exists at the periphery of most religions.)

In contrast, a dedicated and learned Sikh, Buddhist, Muslim, or Jehovah's Witness who believes there is only one way to nirvana, paradise, Allah, or heaven will respectfully say, "Dr. Brad, I know what you believe, but this is what I believe." We would likely part paths agreeing to disagree.

Internationally known scholar and lecturer Ravi Zacharias, born in India and highly knowledgeable of the world's religions, writes, "Truth cannot be all-inclusive. Truth by definition excludes."[31]

He continues: "Anyone who claims that all religions are the same betrays not only an ignorance of all religions but also a caricatured view of even the best-known ones. Every religion at its core is exclusive."[32]

All religions claim exclusivity to some degree. Even those religions that claim to be "all inclusive," allegedly accepting the beliefs of everyone as "truth," still exclude the beliefs of evangelical Christians because of their "one-way" message of salvation.

Pollster George Gallup says that today's trendy religious tolerance is conceived partly by "not only a lack of knowledge of other religions but an ignorance of one's own faith." Some polls, for example, show, "Christians saying, 'Yes, Jesus is the only way' and also, 'Yes, there are many paths to God.' It's not that Americans don't believe anything," reports Gallup, "they believe everything."[33]

Now, some might allege that I'm an arrogant, prejudiced, and hateful person for saying there is only one path to God. But consider this parallel illustration. Suppose you were a patient of mine, sitting in my examining room. Imagine that I walk in with a biopsy report of the large, 3 cm, irregularly contoured, unevenly pigmented, raised skin lesion on your upper arm. Deeply concerned for your well-being, I sit down and gently explain that this lesion on your arm is an aggressive malignant melanoma. "Without a simple surgery to remove it," I say, "you will die."

"I don't believe that," you might respond.

After allowing you to see the telltale biopsy report, I pull a book off my shelf. Flipping to pictures of malignant melanoma skin lesions, I hold the book open for you to see. Gently, I explain further: "According to the biopsy report and valid medical studies, this tumor will eventually spread to organs in your body and kill you if you do not have the simple treatment of surgery."

Now, you might hate me for saying that you have cancer. But what kind of a doctor would I be if I totally ignored your deadly melanoma? Am I an arrogant, prejudiced, and hateful MD for opening my medical textbooks to warn you about the cancer that could bring about your physical death?

You might hate me for saying you have spiritual cancer and that there is only one simple cure for it. But what sort of person would I be if I didn't tenderly warn you about the cancer that will ultimately bring about your spiritual death? Am I not demonstrating my utmost respect and compassion by warning you? If I wouldn't be a prejudiced and narrow-minded doctor for urging surgery as your only cure, how then can I be accused of the same in opening God's Word and urging genuine repentance and faith in God as your only treatment for your spiritual cancer?

For the most part, modern evangelicalism tries to ignore this deadly "melanoma." Caught up in the fashionable swirl of postmodern pseudo-tolerance, many Christians have committed spiritual harlotry in an effort to be friends with the world (see James 4:4). "One way" just isn't cool anymore in a society that tolerates everyone's beliefs as truth.

As a result, tolerance has become falsely equated with love for one's neighbor. But nothing could be further from the truth. This pseudo-tolerance has arisen from the Devil's lie that none of us have this spiritual cancer, that all, or most of us, are "healthy" enough to squeak by into heaven.[34]

But I ask, whose diagnosis will you trust? The diagnosis given by the one true Physician who created you? Or the Devil, whom God labels "a liar and the father of lies" (John 8:44)? Tell me, who is the more loving surgeon? The one who points out the cancer and offers a cure? Or the one who merrily goes about life, totally dismissing the lethal cells that are explosively multiplying in your body and will eventually kill you?

The apostle Peter, filled with the Holy Spirit, proclaimed, "Salvation is found in *no one else*, for there is *no other name* under heaven given to men by which we must be saved" (Acts 4:12). Is the apostle Peter a hateful and vengeful liar for saying that salvation is found only in Jesus Christ? Is Christ an odious and compulsive liar for saying he was the only way to God (see John 14:6)?

Dr. John MacArthur hits the nail on the head:

> In reality, nothing is more *intolerant* than postmodern "tolerance." Postmodernists demand that everyone think alike. They don't believe objective truth exists, and they insist everyone else must also abandon all certainty. Postmodernism has thus enshrined skepticism and made it mandatory.[35]

When it comes to matters such as sin and salvation, God is not a tolerant God, so why should we be tolerant? The church cannot teeter on the world's "tolerance fence" without falling into the abyss of error and chaos.

When King David's days were drawing to a close, he gave this heartfelt advice to his son:

> And you, my son Solomon, acknowledge the God of your
> father, and serve him with wholehearted devotion and with
> a willing mind, for the LORD searches every heart and
> understands every motive behind the thoughts. If you seek
> him, he will be found by you; but if you forsake him, he will
> reject you forever. (1 Chron. 28:9)

You may wonder about people who never hear about God and his
Son, Jesus Christ. Most people know of Helen Keller, the renowned
American author and lecturer who was totally blind and deaf at the age
of two from a debilitating illness. When told a little later in life that
God existed, she replied that she already knew—she just didn't know
his name. Though some of Helen Keller's beliefs did not agree with the
supernatural revelation that comes to us by way of the Bible,[36] this is a
good example of someone recognizing that God exists by way of his
résumé in creation (natural revelation.) Not even the obstacles of blindness and deafness can prevent us from believing that there is a personal
God to whom we are accountable.

The Bible tells us that when God returns, "He will judge the world
with justice, and the nations with fairness" (Psalm 98:9b NLT). We don't
know exactly how God will perform this feat. All we know is that he
promises to be fair according to his own standard of fairness—just as
he is fair in dealing personally with you (see Acts 10:34–35; 17:26–27).

This you can be 100 percent sure of: God will *never* exclude anyone based solely on his or her particular "religious heritage." For truth
is not found in religious tradition—but in God. God has given every
person on earth a copy of his "résumé"—evidence of his existence (see
Rom. 1:20). What we choose to do with this evidence, from our perspective, determines our eternal destinies.

God had a very specific reason for creating mankind. His wise parenting techniques demonstrated and proved, time and again, his
boundless love, his matchless grace, his perfect justice, and his earnest

desire to see us mature into godly men and women—all to his greatest glory.

Throughout this book, we have uncovered many clues that allow us the privilege of gaining a better understanding of our Creator and Lord. These clues, or truths about God, will probably clash with the natural reasoning in our minds and some of our church traditions since birth. But as Dr. Timothy Keller, minister at New York's Redeemer Presbyterian Church tells us, "If you want the *real* God ... you have to be willing to see a God who's going to tell you things you don't want to hear."[37] And while roughly 30 percent of résumés contain outright lies or "inflated" info, we can stand with full assurance and authority on God's "résumé"—his Holy Word—that the *real* God is *exactly* who he says he is in his number one best-selling book of all time.

When it comes to the character of God, maybe a better question to start with is not, "What was God thinking?" but rather, "What are *we* thinking?"

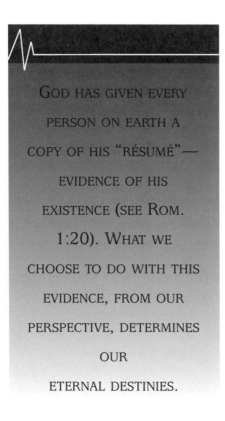

GOD HAS GIVEN EVERY PERSON ON EARTH A COPY OF HIS "RÉSUMÉ"—EVIDENCE OF HIS EXISTENCE (SEE ROM. 1:20). WHAT WE CHOOSE TO DO WITH THIS EVIDENCE, FROM OUR PERSPECTIVE, DETERMINES OUR ETERNAL DESTINIES.

SOLOMON'S CLUE #2

Two small steps forward,
three huge leaps recede.
Heed the differences,
or never succeed.

8

SOLOMON'S CLUES

I have to admit that questions concerning evil and God's sovereignty are not easy questions to crack. That's why there have been tens of thousands of books written throughout history trying to rationalize the two. The reason many fail in their endeavor to figure out the Almighty is that they try to do it "Lone Ranger" style with their Lone Ranger spirituality.[1] God, at best, is often considered a faithful sidekick, much like Tonto, the cinematic Comanche Indian. "You ride on your horse, God, and I'll ride on mine. If I get myself into trouble I'll signal you."

If we ever hope to understand God's sovereignty on the topic of evil, we have to be up close and personal with God on the same "horse." We have to be willing to spend quality time with our heavenly Father in developing a deeper, more intimate relationship. Not in something that resembles a Lone Ranger–Tonto relationship, but like that of an intimate best-friend-and-only-lover, husband-and-wife relationship. This is vitally important to the success of our journey.

To help us in this regard, Solomon has provided us with some very helpful "clues" that will guide us—to the treasures of intimacy with the

WHY DOESN'T GOD STOP EVIL?

divine, leading us to a deep-rooted understanding of the greatest being in the universe. These fictional clues, based on biblical principles, were first presented in another book in this series[†††] after we won $10 million in a bizarre game show. At the end of each book in this series, we will examine one of Solomon's clues in detail for some practical insight into understanding God—as much as our finite minds will allow.

Let's continue in this great quest together....

Snaking along the narrow, racetrack-like country road, I was returning from a speech therapy session. My verbal communication was perfectly fine; it was four-year-old Kierstyn, the adorable little girl of two good friends, who battled an expressive speech disorder. She sat contentedly next to me in the front seat, jabbering away her barely recognizable ABCs, intent on imitating her talking electronic playboard. In the back was her five-year-old brother Samuel, quietly intrigued with the passing scenery of arcadian farmhouses, grazing steeds, and cattail-studded marshes.

I didn't mind volunteering my services as a chauffeur. It was a lovely summer afternoon for a drive. The sky couldn't have been bluer. The trees couldn't have been greener. And the country-fresh smell couldn't have been sweeter. That's why all the windows were down.

Suddenly, my nostrils were lambasted with the most horrid, nauseating stench I'd experienced in a long time. Having grown up in the country, I quickly recognized the foul odor as "eau de skunk."

I reached over instinctively to roll up the windows. Kierstyn, seemingly oblivious, continued with her self-directed speech therapy. But blaring from the backseat came Samuel's excited voice, "Smells like doughnuts!"

Glancing in the rear view mirror I spied Samuel's rosy, beaming cheeks, and wondered which doughnut shop he frequented.

Later I started thinking, "Isn't that just like us as children of God?" To most of us, sin smells like freshly baked doughnuts: a sweet-smelling, tongue-teasing aroma that sumptuously invigorates the senses. Pornography,

---

[†††] *Is God Obsolete?*

extramarital sex, drug abuse, lust, greed, and pride—all seem so inviting, so natural. And the more we smell or taste of it, the more our senses become deadened and accustomed to it. Of course, some of us, like little children, don't even take notice of the foul odor; we're totally oblivious to sin.

But to God, sin is an easily detected, wretched odor—the most repulsive stench to ever attack his senses. Unlike us, God's senses are never deadened by sin. No matter how raunchy or despicable the act, God never becomes accustomed to it. Every vulgar performance we give in his sight is a different, unsullied experience for God. When it comes to sin's daily shows, there are no mind-numbing reruns for the Divine.

John Piper wrote, "Sin is like spiritual leprosy. It deadens your spiritual senses so that you rip your soul to shreds and don't even feel it."[2] Often patients with leprosy or severe diabetes will develop ulcers on the bottom of their feet because they lack the normal feeling most people enjoy. Through time, their skin breaks down. Dead tissue, and sometimes pus, will cover over the wound edges, preventing the healthy cells from joining together to close the ulcer. On several occasions I've had to debride (cut away) the dead tissue in a diabetic's foot as a family member or third-year medical student looked on in horror. They couldn't believe that I would be cutting away on someone's foot with a scalpel without using some kind of anesthetic. Most of the time the patient just leaned back as if he were having his toenails trimmed. "Feel anything?" I would politely ask—more in an attempt to relieve everyone's fears. "No," was the usual reply. I knew when I cut into healthy tissue: usually not by any scream, but by the presence of bleeding.

As Piper says, "Sin is like spiritual leprosy." It removes the "feeling" in your spiritual senses so that basically anything can cut into your extremities and you won't feel it. By the time the pain reaches the core of your being, it's too late. The damage has been done, and chances are, your life—and perhaps your relationship with God—will never be the same again.

Willfully living in the sins of pride, greed, deceit, and lust, and trying to understand God on our journey, is like taking two tiny steps forward at best, then three giant leaps backward. When our spiritual senses are deadened, our spiritual vision becomes clouded, causing us to often choose the wrong path—making it almost impossible to understand the mysterious qualities of God. Oh sure, we may be drawn to God in spite of our evil-doings. God has reached down and pulled up numerous alcoholics, prostitutes, wife beaters, and hardened convicts when they couldn't go much lower (see Eph. 2:4–6). But during the actual foreplay and inter-course of our iniquities, we drift farther away from God our Savior. "Deadened spiritual senses" is just one of the many differences that drive us apart from our Maker.

We've briefly contrasted the captivating beauty of God's holiness with the ugly dullness of our cracked beings. In the other books in the series we'll examine in more detail the disparity between divine justice and mortal "justice." And we'll see more clearly that we can't compete with the omniscience, omnipresence, immutability, eternity, transcen-dence, and awesomeness of our majestic God.

But why is it so important to heed the differences?

An in-depth understanding of the person of God requires true inti-macy. This is very, very important on our journey. Imagine how much understanding would exist in a marriage relationship if physical, emo-tional, and spiritual intimacy did not exist. To develop a proper understanding of God, we must also share an intimate relationship with him. And to do that, it is essential that we first recognize and accept the differences that exist between our Creator and us.

Many couples become mutually attracted because of differences: an off-the-wall personality, an appealing intelligence, an outgoing demeanor, or an affluent socioeconomic background. "Opposites attract," is a com-mon catchphrase for a common phenomenon. Could this be one reason why young children are so captivated by God? Does the complete pack-age of a big, all-powerful, all-knowing, and all-loving deity somehow fulfill the inadequacies of their lives? I think to some extent it does.

But then we grow up. And these differences, which at one time attracted us to God, now drive us away. We resent an all-knowing and all-wise God because we think we know best. We begrudge an all-powerful God because we want to do everything on our own. We are even somewhat offended by a loving God because our love can never match up to his. Studies show that couples with the most differences have the stormiest marriages.[3] Those who cannot accept, and live with, the majestic perfections of God, also have the rockiest relationships with their Creator.

Gary Smalley, one of the world's leading experts on love and relationships, wrote a book titled, *Secrets to Lasting Love: Uncovering the Keys to Life-Long Intimacy.*[4] In it, Smalley describes five levels of intimacy to help couples move into, what he calls, "The ultimate level of intimacy."[5]

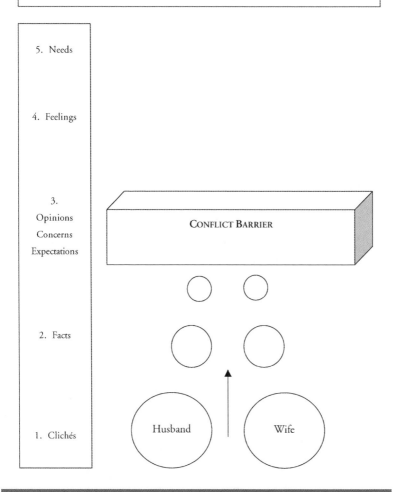

THE FIVE LEVELS OF INTIMACY By Gary Smalley

5. Needs

4. Feelings

3. Opinions Concerns Expectations

CONFLICT BARRIER

2. Facts

1. Clichés

Husband

Wife

WHY DOESN'T GOD STOP EVIL?

Interestingly, there are several good parallels we can draw to our own relationship with God. Take a close look at Smalley's "Five levels of Intimacy." Now, substitute "God" and "Us" for "Husband" and "Wife."

Leaving everything else the same, we notice that we are separated from God when our relationship is built on the *first* level: clichés. In a rocky marriage, communication is limited to a passing, "How are you?" "Nice weather, huh?" and "Have a good day." With God, we may routinely utter the words, "God is love," "Thy will be done," and "O Holy God of matchless grace." We might even publicly recite the Lord's Prayer every Sunday morning in church, but that's the limit of our superficial acquaintance with the Divine.

The *second* level involves uncovering facts, or the stepping-stones, about God (see *Is God Obsolete?*). But this still leaves us separated from him. In a strained marriage, communication is usually limited to gaining and sharing mundane facts:

"Did you get the groceries?"

"Yeah."

"What did you do today?"

"The muffler fell off, so I took the car into the shop and picked the lint out of my belly-button for half an hour."

With God, we sit in a church service and frequently hear the preacher elaborate on the charm of our "Cosmic Pal." But our lackluster friendship with our Creator is still a "water-cooler" relationship, where we impersonally come together with God during our breaks to chat about our kids and fill him in on what's happening in our lives.

The *third* level in the husband-wife relationship is what Smalley terms the conflict barrier. This is where we meet God head on—sharing all our opinions, concerns, and expectations of whom we believe God is and how we think he should conduct himself. According to Smalley, "an estimated 50 percent of American couples are prisoners behind the wall of conflict."[6] Like half of all marriages, an equally high percentage of parishioners in Christian churches likely never break past this barrier. A personal, intimate relationship with their heavenly Father never becomes a reality.

Why does this barrier exist? For the same reason many Hollywood couples say they divorce: *irreconcilable differences*.

With regard to a marriage relationship, Smalley writes:

> Once you make the decision to honor and validate your mate's differences, you can step inside his or her room [that person's world]. Why? Because you're no longer threatened by the differences that define him or her, differences that once had the power to make you feel like you had to be on the defensive.[7]

Why do so many people in this world lack an intimate understanding of the Divine? It's because they can't accept the differences that exist between themselves and God. They can't stomach a God who is so utterly holy and perfectly just that he punishes sin. They can't handle a God who demands complete faithfulness in a marriage-like relationship. They jump on the defensive every time these differences erupt. Why? Because we are like night and day compared to God's character. We don't want to admit that we're sinners who pain God every day. And we don't want anyone, especially our Creator, telling us that we can't be like him—as little gods ourselves.

Consequently, spiritual seekers do something married couples do all the time: "They try to eliminate the differences that define them, and in doing so they emotionally suffocate their mates and stray from the path of intimacy."[8] To eliminate the differences, to reduce God to our level, God's holiness is often watered down, turning him into an all-loving divine pushover. Consequently, true spiritual intimacy with God is never experienced, and an understanding of the Creator remains pathetically limited.

Heed the differences, or never succeed. Once we make "the decision to honor and validate" God's differences—particularly God's holiness and his justice—we are making this life-long commitment to God in our hearts:

> I admit that we have many differences, but these differences will no longer be a point of contention, but instead a place for greater understanding.[9]

Let God be God, and I guarantee, you'll have much less difficulty understanding your Creator.

WHY DOESN'T GOD STOP EVIL?

THE MASTER KEY

En route to triumph, the cup is held out;
Drink to discover, beyond any doubt.

Precedence and awe, intimacy great,
The secret is yours, push open the gate.

Once through the blockade, the world is anew,
But never lodge here, regrets if you do.

The further you go, the further you taste.
To share is the proof—to fear is a waste.

—SOLOMON'S CLUES #3–6

Let's continue with Solomon's helpful clues, helping us to understand better these five levels of intimacy. We are all made in God's image, so it only makes sense that the relationship skills needed for a successful marriage will be somewhat similar to the ones needed for an intimate relationship with God.

We've already discussed how our connection with the Divine is a "puppy love" relationship when it is built on clichés and facts (e.g., merely reciting the Lord's Prayer every day). We've also come to learn the importance of acknowledging and accepting God's differences from us (e.g., his holiness, justice, and majesty); if we don't accept these differences, then we have no hope for an intimate relationship with God.

Solomon's third clue, "En route to triumph the cup is held out; Drink to discover, beyond any doubt," emphasizes for us this truth: without drinking from the cup of salvation offered to us by Christ, we have no hope of uncovering the deepest mysteries of God. We cannot have any degree of intimacy with God until we first accept Christ's sacrifice on the cross as full payment for our sins, repent of our sins, and commit our lives to him. For when we accept the cup of salvation, the Holy Spirit (the third member of the trinity) takes up permanent residence in our bodies to help us properly arrange our stepping-stones around the really tough questions about God. Without God indwelling us, we have no hope for intimacy.

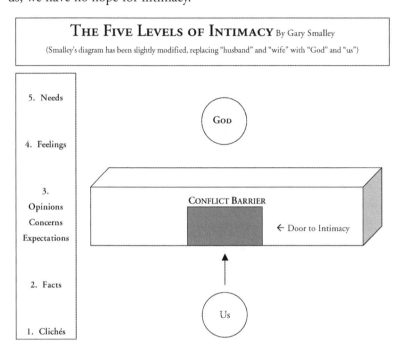

THE FIVE LEVELS OF INTIMACY By Gary Smalley

(Smalley's diagram has been slightly modified, replacing "husband" and "wife" with "God" and "us")

5. Needs

4. Feelings

3. Opinions Concerns Expectations

2. Facts

1. Clichés

GOD

CONFLICT BARRIER

← Door to Intimacy

Us

The next of Solomon's clues reads, "Precedence and awe, intimacy great, The secret is yours, push open the gate." This clue emphasizes the need for *commitment* in our relationship with God. Before we can push open the gate to intimacy, we must first unlock it with the proper key. Where can we find this one and only key? Listen to what Smalley says in regard to human relationships:

> Without honor, you cannot attain intimacy.... Honor has to be the center of the relationship....[10] *Honor opens the door to the fourth and fifth levels of intimacy.* And it's a master key.[11]

Another relationship expert, Dr. John Gottman, writes, "You can learn all the marriage skills you want, but without reverence, awe, respect, and admiration (other terms for honor) it doesn't work."[12]

WHY DOESN'T GOD STOP EVIL?

This couldn't be any truer of our relationship with God. We *must* have genuine reverence, awe, respect, and appreciation; otherwise we remain helplessly stuck as only shallow acquaintances with the Almighty.

To honor your spouse is to have tremendous respect for his or her individual qualities and differences.[13] Yet it goes even a step further than this; it also involves a crucial element lacking in so many marriages today: *honor*. Honor, insists Smalley, requires giving "priority status" to your mate.[14] Those people who refuse to give God "priority status" in their lives will never achieve true intimacy, and consequently will never achieve an in-depth understanding of the Almighty. Solomon wrote, "The fear of the LORD is the beginning of knowledge" (Prov. 1:7). Without a healthy fear of God, the mind cannot know and the heart cannot understand the infinite depths of God's marvelous perfections (see 1 Cor. 2:14; Eph. 1:18).

This is what separates a "nametag" or cultural Christian from a true Christian—a true follower of Christ. The cultural Christian never breaks through the conflict barrier because he or she fails to genuinely honor God—to totally submit every aspect of life to him. Cultural Christians have not come to terms with the hidden sins of the heart that separate them from God. Their pride and "morals" hinder them from accepting God's offer of salvation through his Son, Jesus Christ. And they refuse to truly honor God by giving him their lives and drinking from the cup of salvation.

Lest you misunderstand me here, giving God "priority status" does not mean making it to church every Sunday—or becoming a monk. Making God the highest priority requires an attitude of submission in every aspect of our daily lives. It involves seeking God's moral will and giving God the glory in everything we do: our work, marriages, churches, leisure time, thoughts, and aspirations. It involves denying our own self-interests to place God's desires above ours. It involves a whole-hearted, dedicated effort to following God's divine guidelines—not our own. Paul Johnson, the Catholic author of *The Quest for God*, writes, "There can be no peace of mind for us on the subject of eternal damnation without a total submission to God's will."[15]

Some spiritual seekers drop out prematurely from the search: "I tried Christianity, I tried God and it didn't work," they proclaim.[16] What these seekers are really saying is this: "I wanted something, but God didn't give it to me."[17] Honoring someone, as in a marriage relationship, involves sacrificially giving—not selfishly getting. Honoring God is not about what I can get out of the Divine Father in the way of heaven or financial windfalls. Genuine honor involves giving over the throne of our lives to God, as he rightfully deserves. As Dr. Keller correctly points out, "Religious people find God useful; Christians find God beautiful."[18]

Unlike these dropout spiritual seekers, some self-proclaimed Christians shun the "good works" path, but they still cling to their illusionary faith. A surprising number of people are selfishly obsessed with only eternal self-preservation. The thought of spending an eternity in hell has terrorized them so much, they rambled off the "sinner's prayer" without humbly acknowledging that they are actually sinners.

Now, this may strike a heavy blow to some of you, but if your *only* motive for saying yes to God was to escape hell—if you have never genuinely repented of your sins and accepted Christ's sacrifice on the cross as payment for your sins—then you have not given God priority status in your life; you don't possess a genuine godly fear; you don't understand how much your sins pain God; you are not a true Christian; you are not a "new creature" (see 2 Cor. 5:17); you have no relationship with God whatsoever; and ironically, you are just as much on your way to hell as you were before. Such is the tragic by-product of modern evangelicalism, where "signing up for Jesus" is always stressed, but true commitment and repentance are rarely mentioned. "But unless you repent," warned Christ, "you too will all perish" (Luke 13:5).

The difference between a religious or cultural Christian clutching a *hollow faith*, and a true, devoted follower of Christ, possessing *true faith*, is intimacy with the Divine: *an instrumental God who is there (in heaven)—versus a beautiful God who is here (in our hearts).*[19] The religious Christians may ritualistically pay homage to the great God up above, but the true Christians worship, in an attitude of humble submission, the personal God who dwells within them, controlling key areas of their lives.

WHY DOESN'T GOD STOP EVIL?

The difference is closeness—intimacy that can only be achieved by genuine repentance and acceptance of Christ's work on the cross as payment for our sins (see Acts 17:30; Rom. 10:9; 2 Cor. 7:10).

HOPELESSLY STUCK

Solomon's fifth clue reads, "Once through the blockade, the world is anew; But never lodge here, regrets if you do."

How often has a believer enthusiastically broken through the conflict barrier to God—attending every Bible study possible, witnessing to the lost, trekking half way around the world on mission trips—only to remain helplessly stuck, or lodged, in the pursuit of further intimacy with the Divine? We try our best to give priority status to God; but for some reason our relationship with our Creator never progresses to the fourth and fifth levels—"the ultimate level of intimacy," as Smalley calls it.

What's going on here?

The word *lodge* is the key to this clue. In the Old Testament *lodge* comes from the Hebrew *lun* or *liyn*, which means to remain, dwell, or tarry. But these Hebrew words have a second important meaning: *to grumble, complain, or murmur*. Do you think it's just a coincidence that the same Hebrew word can mean either *lodge* or *grumble?*

What happens in a marriage relationship when one or both partners kick start the grumbling machinery into motion? The husband lashes out at his wife, "Why can't you ever have dinner ready for me when it's your turn to cook?" To which the wife responds, "I work too, you know. You never have the decency to call and let me know when you'll be home. I'm not a psychic. How am I supposed to know your estimated time of arrival?"

The couple might grumble about each other's handling of finances, each other's inability to satisfy certain sexual needs, raising the kids, and so forth. What happens, though, to the couple's relationship from all this grumbling? They become "lodged" or "stuck" in their pursuit of intimacy. How can one possibly cultivate an intimate understanding of someone if he or she is constantly grumbling about the other person's actions?

And so it is in our relationship with God. When we grumble to God about our jobs, our financial situation, our health, our spouses, all the evil and suffering in the world, what we're really saying is, "God, you don't know what you're doing! C'mon! Get your act together!"

Now you might respond, "I don't grumble to God." The Bible character Rachel (Jacob's wife) might have said the same thing. Instead of complaining directly to God, whom did she complain to?

> When Rachel saw that she wasn't having any children, she became jealous of her sister. "Give me children, or I'll die!" she exclaimed to Jacob. Jacob flew into a rage. "Am I God?" he asked. "He is the only one able to give you children!" (Gen. 30:1–2 NLT)

Often we turn our bitterness and rage against others when things aren't going our way. What we're really doing though, is questioning God's competency in running the universe. When the Israelites grumbled to Moses and Aaron about the food shortage, Moses rebuked them, "Who are we? You are not grumbling against us, but against the LORD" (Ex. 16:8b). Attacking others is just our way of unleashing our hatred and disgust at God. There's really no difference—except that we end up destroying two relationships instead of one.

Murmuring or complaining is also a sign of blatant ungratefulness. We become ungrateful when God seems to shun our "mangos" by removing his "magic seeds" of grace in our lives—something we didn't deserve in the first place. No matter what or to whom we grumble, when we get right down to it, the root of grumbling is questioning the wisdom and graciousness of God. And it's a dangerous place to be.

Grumbling is also a mark of absolute selfishness. It's saying, "God, *I* don't care what would bring the most glory to your name. *I* want this career. *I* want to date this man or this woman. *I* want to own this car. *I* want to live in that house. *I* want this, *I* want that, *I* want…." God welcomes our prayer requests, yet often he must feel like a beleaguered, unpaid day-care worker listening to a bunch of children whine about what they're not getting.

I don't care how many verses you memorize, how many hours you spend meditating, or how long you read or study the Bible, if you are constantly grumbling to God, or others, you will *never* progress another step in your understanding of the Almighty. Grumbling will get you nowhere. If you are keeping the grumbling machinery in motion, you might as well close up this book because you will never grow in your understanding of God.

Stop for a moment and carefully examine your life. Are there grumbling thoughts swishing around in your mind? Maybe a neighbor whose dog is inappropriately fertilizing your lawn? Maybe a boss who won't give you a promotion? A spouse who doesn't want you to start up your own business? A bank that won't help you out with your credit-card debt? A school board that won't provide more funding for your disabled child? A surgeon who won't perform the operation you want? Have you ever stopped to think that God may actually be using the particular animals or people in these circumstances to somehow advance his kingdom?

I admit, there are many times when life doesn't make very much sense. Physical suffering, job losses, a child's death, divorce, terrorist attacks—we gaze upon these terrible circumstances and tragedies in our lives through the narrow lens and wonder why God would allow them to occur. If you had been the teenager Joseph in biblical times, watching your mother die, being sold into slavery by your brothers and then unfairly tossed into prison, it would have been easy to question the wisdom of God. Yet we never read once of Joseph grumbling to his Maker.

I shamefully confess that I have grumbled at God on several occasions. I grumbled when I was invited to try out at a provincial junior "A" hockey team, but didn't make it.[20] I complained when I had to wait three years, instead of two, before being accepted to medical school. I moped around when a certain person of the opposite sex wouldn't return my phone calls. I resentfully questioned God when I couldn't sell my first two film screenplays. Several times I have griped at God for something or other. From my perspective, my "mangos" were just as nice as anyone's.

Looking back on my life, though, I can plainly see God's wisdom in *not* giving me what I wanted. I once heard a pastor say, "You don't *want* what you *want*." How true that has been in my life. Had God granted my wish on the spot for a certain wife, a particular medical school, a hockey career, or screenwriting success, the chances are great that I wouldn't be writing these books.

Without a doubt, the greatest moments of understanding and intimacy with my heavenly Father came when I stopped grumbling. That doesn't mean I became a doormat and passively allowed life to be dumped on me. No, it meant acquiring the wisdom from God to know what things could be changed and turning everything over into his hands.

"To criticize God's wisdom only shows one's own ignorance," writes Dr. Roy B. Zuck. "The chasm between God and man leaves no place for pride and self-sufficiency."[21] Instead of grumbling about this and that, doesn't it make more sense to praise God that he is in control and not we?

Not even Solomon could fully understand God's mysterious ways:

> A man's steps are directed by the LORD. How then can anyone understand his own way? (Prov. 20:24)

Believing that God's choices in life are always perfect means accepting that whatever event befalls me fits perfectly into God's divine purposes. No matter how ugly the mosaic piece may look through the narrow lens, we must accept by faith that the entire mosaic brings the most glory to God. When you reach heaven, I promise that you'll be able to spot all of God's footprints and trace all the markers (or signposts) of God's trail in history and throughout your life. And you'll be able to see, through God's wider lens, the most beautiful mosaic you've ever laid eyes on.

GO AHEAD: TELL GOD HOW YOU FEEL

Solomon's sixth clue is, "The further you go, the further you taste. To share is the proof—to fear is a waste."

In our quest for intimacy with the Divine, we move onto the fourth level of intimacy: *feelings*. According to the relationship expert Gary Smalley, a couple has reached the fourth level of intimacy when they are able to honestly share their deepest feelings without fear. A wife might disclose, "Honey, I'm feeling neglected and unimportant over how little time you're spending with me." A wife who wasn't sure if her husband really loved her would not likely share such a personal feeling for fear of retaliation and driving her husband even further away (unless, of course, she didn't care whether her husband stuck around). Only when two partners can freely share their feelings in a nonthreatening atmosphere of love can there be true intimacy.

When it comes to our relationship with God, the same principle generally holds true (refer to the diagram above). When we know that our God of infinite goodness truly loves us, we are not afraid to share any of our deepest feelings. But in today's popular emotion-based faith, stepping-stones are often arranged in accordance with one's shifting *feelings* of God—rather than with the enduring *truth* of God. Consequently, when our feelings suddenly change and clash with our stepping-stones, we are forced to either change our understanding of God (something that's very difficult to do) or try to suppress our feelings (something that's equally difficult—and harmful).

For example, the person who believes that a good God will always heal when petitioned will quickly grow angry if a loved one suddenly dies of an illness like cancer or heart disease. Such a person must either stifle those angry feelings by breaking off communication with God or quickly rearrange the stepping-stones. He or she has come to the conclusion that God isn't always good or that God isn't powerful enough to prevent evil, as did Rabbi Kushner, author of *Why Bad Things Happen to Good People,* when his son died.

In stark contrast, the person who enjoys an intimate relationship with God will always be honest with God. Why? Because such a person knows the true character of God and is not afraid of sharing the feelings—whether negative or positive. Such a person will pray, "God, you know how much my heart is aching right now, and you know how angry I am that you allowed my loved one to die. But I realize my feelings are deceiving me because they are not based on the truth of who you are. For you are a sovereign God who is just and fair—the Lord who is my Shepherd, who I can always trust to be good and work all things out for your glory—even if I can't always understand it. I know that it is only by your undeserved grace that any of us are still alive." It doesn't take long for the feelings of anger to disappear.

Pastors, both young and old, will often harbor feelings of guilt and discouragement over low attendance and few conversions in their congregations. But the pastor who truly understands God will pray, "God, you know that I'm feeling discouraged over the lack of success; and I have to confess that I am a little resentful right now; but Lord, I know that if I and my entrusted fold put you first in our lives, you will spiritually bless us beyond our expectations. And I understand, God, that you are not someone who measures success by the world's standards—but by your own blessed standards." It doesn't take long for feelings of shame, discouragement, and resentment to disappear.

The intimacy we share with God allows us to see those feelings for what they are: *shifting emotions centered on the circumstances at hand.* We understand that God is not those circumstances. Just because we're having a bad day, does not mean that God is too. Just because we're feeling that God is a thousand miles away does not mean he is. If you let your feelings hijack your mind, manipulate your heart, and in the process, warp your understanding of God, you will never progress another step in your drive for intimacy with the Divine.

Only those with a very intimate or a very shallow relationship with God will openly communicate their feelings without trying to suppress them in any way. Those in an intimate relationship know God and know that their feelings, though very real, are not an accurate determination of who God is (see Phil. 1:9). In the opposite corner are those who possess a shallow relationship, with little understanding of God. They will openly vent their anger or bitterness because they don't care if God sticks around or not. They've had it with the Almighty, who doesn't seem to be fulfilling his end of the bargain. (Actually, such individuals rarely get past the conflict barrier to the fourth level of intimacy because their fanciful expectations of the Almighty keep them continually chained in a shallow or nonexistent relationship.)

Believers stuck somewhere in between the rungs on the intimacy ladder are often afraid to share their deepest feelings when life goes awry: "Either I've failed or God has failed," they believe. Most will eventually lean toward the latter, too ashamed to tell anyone.

WHY DOESN'T GOD STOP EVIL?

Maybe you haven't thought much about it, but God openly shares his feelings too. For instance, he shared with Moses just how angry he was with the children of Israel: "Now leave me alone so that my anger may burn" (Ex. 32:10). We read in Psalm 147:11 that "the LORD delights [enjoys, is pleased, finds greater pleasure] in those who fear him, who put their hope in his unfailing love." He also shares with us in the pages of Genesis how "his heart was filled with pain" when he looked down on the wickedness of mankind (Gen. 6:6).

But we must never forget, as J. I. Packer reminds us, "God feels—though in a way of necessity that transcends a finite being's experience of emotion."[22] The way in which we experience human emotions (love, hate, happiness, grief, anger etc.) cannot be purely applied to the way our God "feels" (see Ps. 50:21).

Packer also points out "God's feelings are not beyond his control, as ours often are."[23] Since God's feelings arise from the whole of his transcendent, unchanging, all-knowing, and all-seeing character, our Shepherd's feelings are as rational as two plus two. In comparison, our feelings are often irrational, and difficult to control because they are frequently centered on our desires or on false beliefs (such as with the bitter person who falsely believes that God *owes* her or him a long and healthy life).

Should feelings play any role in our special relationship with our Good Shepherd? Of course![24] As John Piper adamantly insists in his book *Desiring God*, strong emotions certainly have their place: "Truth without emotion produces dead orthodoxy and a church full (or half-full) of artificial admirers.... On the other hand," he warns, "emotion without truth produces empty frenzy and cultivates shallow people who refuse the discipline of rigorous thought.... Strong affections for God rooted in truth are the bone and marrow of biblical worship."[25] Feelings are an integral part of any intimate relationship—including a relationship with God; they must, however, arise from the truth of who God is; we must never pluck "truth" out of our emotions and feelings.

"For the word of God is living and active. Sharper than any double-edged sword, it penetrates even to dividing soul and spirit, joints and marrow" (Heb. 4:12). When the word of God pierces this deeply into our needy spirits and our hungry souls, we can't help but experience overwhelming feelings of sweetness, burning, sorrow, tears, laughter, joy, and delight. The truth about God can reduce the most powerful person to tears, or it can bring joy to the poorest, sickest, most depraved human being in the filthiest ghetto.

In his popular book *Knowing God* J. I. Packer writes:

> Knowing God is a matter of *personal involvement*, in mind, will and feeling.
>
> [It's] an emotional relationship, as well as an intellectual and volitional one, and could not indeed be a deep relation between persons were it not so.[26]

"How sweet are your words to my taste," writes the psalmist, "sweeter than honey to my mouth!" (Ps. 119:103). "Taste and see that the Lord is good; blessed is the man who takes refuge in him" (Ps. 34:8). To taste of God is to experience one-of-a-kind intimacy with our loving heavenly Father, whom we personally and deeply know (see John 10:14–15).

The proof that we have attained the fourth level of intimacy is our openness in sharing our feelings with God ... along with our sincerity in listening to God communicate his feelings to us in his Word. Never should we feel as though we are walking on eggshells with the Lord, too afraid to confess our deepest feelings. God our Father affectionately listens to our feelings and our prayers; if we want to build an intimate relationship with our Creator we must, in turn, take the time to listen to his feelings and his desires.

In a one-sided relationship, intimacy is only a dispiriting illusion.

> But let him who boasts boast about this: that he understands and knows me. (Jer. 9:24)

SCENES FROM
THE JOURNEY AHEAD

In the other books in this series, we dig even deeper into some of the richest, most profound, and most life-changing areas of God's character. Some of the most original and provocative material awaits you in the books to come.

Here's a quick look at the other books in An MD Examines:

IS GOD OBSOLETE?

Nearly everyone at some point in life questions God's ability to run the universe. But are we asking the proper questions, from the proper perspective, based on a proper understanding of the Almighty? What might we have in common with a four-year-old? You might be surprised to discover the similarities as we explore the "personal spirituality" craze overtaking the world. Has God become, in a sense, obsolete? This book in the series is packed with gripping anecdotes and lively illustrations—from trying to resuscitate a gangbanger's exposed heart, to participating in one of the most bizarre futuristic game shows ever concocted. This minibook is a great resource to pass along to believers and nonbelievers alike.

DOES GOD STILL DO MIRACLES?

Much debate lingers over the hot questions: Is God still performing miracles of healing today? If so, how common are they? Many Christian physicians, including me, believe God still performs miracles of physical healing that defy natural explanation. But are the hosts of "miracles" we hear about so often truly miracles? If these faith healings are not true miracles, then how does one explain the thousands of people who are instantaneously getting better? If the diseases being "cured" are not "all in one's head," then what biological mechanisms could possibly explain this phenomenon we're seeing? Why not just give God the benefit of the doubt and label every astonishing healing a miracle? What insights does God provide us in his Word? This book takes seriously Paul's mandate to "examine everything carefully" (1 Thess. 5:21 NASB). Some of the most fascinating and up-to-date medical and investigative research is examined in an attempt to uncover the truth about what is going on in faith-healing services and healing shrines around the world. A new generation of believers wants answers—and *Does God Still Do Miracles?* delivers.

WHY DOES GOD ALLOW SUFFERING?

In this book we'll use the insight and understanding gained from other books in the series to help us answer one of the toughest questions ever asked of the Almighty: How can a God of love allow his children to suffer? Several inspiring true stories are presented, including the stirring account of how Steven Curtis Chapman faced the "thunder and lightning" in his life. This book goes further than most books on suffering by using illustrations and analogies to help the reader better understand the root cause of why we suffer. It also contains a unique story that helps us understand the real question at the heart of the matter: How can God be altogether just, kind, holy, righteous, and loving in the midst of our suffering? (See Jer. 9:24.)

At the end of each book we'll continue to examine a part of Solomon's fictional clues for some vital and practical insight into our Creator. By doing so, we'll break past the conflict barrier to illustrate the five levels of intimacy with our heavenly Father. And as always, we won't give up no matter how treacherous the waters, how yawning the valleys, or how lofty the mountains. An understanding of God will radically affect our lives like nothing else!

READERS' GUIDE
FOR PERSONAL REFLECTION OR GROUP DISCUSSION

CHAPTER 1
SCRUTINIZING THE RÉSUMÉ

1. Consider the illustration that opens this chapter. Have you ever thought about God in similar terms? How is this illustration like God's relation to us, and how is it different?
2. What is our greatest hindrance to properly understanding God?
3. What is meant by "the openness of God"? What do you think about this idea? Do you think it accurately describes God? Why or why not?
4. According to the author, what are the four "job qualities for sovereign ruler"? What do these things say about God?

CHAPTER 2
WHAT ABOUT MY MANGOS?

1. The author states that God is in complete control of everything in the universe, including human beings. Does that mean God is the author of evil? If God permits evil, does that mean he's responsible for it? What do you think about the author's illustrations regarding this point?
2. Do you think it's possible to overstress the sovereignty of God? If God can foresee evil, doesn't that mean he's responsible for it? What do you make of the illustration of the "white miracle doctor"? How does it apply to the question of God's sovereignty?
3. What is the only thing our heavenly Father gives us that we don't deserve? What was God's greatest display of grace and goodness?

READERS' GUIDE

CHAPTER 3
QUESTIONING THE WHIRLWIND

1. What example of supposedly evil behavior does the author give that is often regarded as relative from different perspectives? What ways have you seen people in your own life view morality from different perspectives? Isn't this moral relativism?
2. Instead of asking what we think about evil, what is a better question to ask? Is God's judgment of evil always fair? Give reasons for your answer.
3. Why is God's judgment termed "retaliatory"? With what did God replace his retaliatory judgment?
4. What is God's indirect judgment? What is his direct judgment? How do they differ? What can happen to us if we ignore the difference between God's direct and indirect judgment?

CHAPTER 4
SPILLING THE GOODS ON EVIL

1. What are some of the ways God has kept the lid on evil down through the ages? What does this show about God's nature?
2. What are some of the reasons God allows the tragic consequences to unfold in this world? What would happen to us if "we got what we deserve"?
3. If there were no consequences for sin in the world, what would that do to the hearts of men and women?

CHAPTER 5
WHERE WAS GOD ON SEPTEMBER 11?

1. Is it possible for us to know for sure why God allowed 9/11? Why or why not?
2. What does the author think about the idea that 9/11 was a judgment on America? What reasons does he give for his view? Do you agree or disagree?
3. What do you make of Anne Lotz's explanation of where God was on 9/11?
4. Instead of asking why millions of people died in the flood, were killed by Joshua, or died on 9/11, what question should we be asking? How does Luke 13:1–5 fit in here?
5. What does the author say is the real reason for why God allowed three thousand people to die on 9/11? Do you agree or disagree? Why or why not?

WHY DOESN'T GOD STOP EVIL?

CHAPTER 6
HURRICANE KATRINA: GOD'S DIVINE AGENDA?

1. Which do you think is more surprising about Hurricane Katrina: the bungled rescue efforts, or the fact that a hurricane of such devastating force hadn't struck New Orleans earlier?
2. Why, as someone who has spent his entire adult life in the medical field, does the author say doctors seldom ask the question, "Where was God when such and such disaster struck?"
3. What is God's message in these tragedies? Why do you think it's so difficult, even for many Christians, to get the right message from disasters like Hurricane Katrina? According to the author, why does God sometimes rock our world in an uncomfortable way?

CHAPTER 7
THE TOUGHEST QUESTIONS ABOUT GOD

1. Why are God's wise decisions usually not the most popular decisions with the world's populace?
2. Why do you think evil exists? Does the author's explanation fit with yours? Why or why not?
3. If you have questions about God that are more difficult to answer than the ones discussed in this book, what are they? How can you begin to find answers to them?
4. What answer does the author give to the question about there being only one way of salvation? How does his answer relate to the issue of millions of people never having heard the gospel?

CHAPTER 8
SOLOMON'S CLUES

1. What are some proper and improper ways of learning about God's sovereignty and the problem of evil? Have you ever run across a book or books on these topics that you felt were wrongly oriented toward these questions?
2. What does author John Piper compare sin to? In relation to the author's description of debriding diabetic foot ulcers on some of his patients, can you identify with this analogy or not? Why or why not?
3. Where on the five levels of intimacy are you with God? If you desire to go up a level or two, what would facilitate that process in your life?
4. According to the author, why do so many people lack an intimate understanding of the Divine? What do spiritual seekers do to try to remedy this lack? Why doesn't this strategy work? What do they need to do instead?

APPENDIX: SET FREE?

*Because through Christ Jesus the law of
the Spirit of life set me free from the
law of sin and death.*

—ROMANS 8:2

Some interpret this verse to mean that we, as true believers, are set free from the *physical* curse of the law of sin and death, meaning that we are free from all manner of sickness and disease. But from the context, Paul is not talking about the *physical* laws, but rather the *spiritual* laws of sin and death. Paul clarifies the meaning of verse 2 in verse 10 of the same chapter: "But if Christ is in you, your body is dead because of sin, yet your spirit is alive because of righteousness." Paul also writes, "What a wretched man I am! Who will rescue me from this body of death?" (Rom. 7:24). He's saying that we are set free from the bondage of our sin nature and eternal death—*not physical death*. If Christ were to literally set us free from the physical effects of the law of sin and death, then no believer would age, become sick, or die. Obviously this is not the case. Again, you cannot separate the disease process from the physical process of aging and death.

Christ will one day set us completely free from our mortal "body of death" and redeem our "perishable" bodies—but not until the final day of redemption (see Rom. 8:11, 23; 1 Cor. 15:42–44; Phil. 3:20–21; Rev. 21:4).

NOTES

INTRODUCTION
A RÉSUMÉ UNLIKE ANY OTHER

1. For more discussion on the "gravitational time dilation" theory, see "How Can We See Distant Stars in a Young Universe" in Ken Ham, Jonathan Sarfati, and Carl Wieland, *The Revised & Expanded Answers Book*, ed. Don Batten (Green Forest, AR: Master Books, 2000), 95–102. For a scientific review of creation and astronomy see Danny R. Faulkner, "The Current State of Creation Astronomy" (presented at the Fourth International Conference on Creationism, Pittsburgh, PA, August 3–8, 1998), http://www.icr.org/research/df/df-r01.htm (accessed March 7, 2003).

CHAPTER 1
SCRUTINIZING THE RÉSUMÉ

1. Allison Adato and Miriam Bensimhon, "Features/Life Special: Kids' Pictures to God," *Life*, March 1, 1998, 68.
2. John Piper, *Desiring God: Meditations of a Christian Hedonist*, 10th Anniversary Expanded Edition (Sisters, OR: Multnomah Books, 1986), 42.

3. Ibid. (emphasis in original).
4. Ibid., 39.
5. Richard Swenson, "More Than Meets the Eye," *Physician*, July/August 2001, 7, as quoted in Richard Swenson, *More Than Meets the Eye* (Colorado Springs: Navpress, 2000).
6. John Calvin, *The Knowledge of God the Creator: Book One of the Institutes of the Christian Religion*, Henry Beveridge, trans., (Grand Rapids, MI: Douma Publications, n.d.), 194.
7. Charles R. Swindoll, *The Mystery of God's Will* (Nashville: W Publishing Group, 1999), 87.
8. Ibid.
9. As quoted in Arthur W. Pink, *Gleanings in the Godhead* (Chicago: Moody Press, 1975), 31.
10. John MacArthur, *Can God Bless America?* (Nashville: W Publishing Group, 2002), vi.
11. John MacArthur, "Is Israel's Unbelief Inconsistent with God's Plan?" (Grace To You, 1983), tape GC 45-71.
12. Stephen Charnock, *The Existence and Attributes of God* (Minneapolis: Klock & Klock, 1977), 719.
13. According to a study conducted by Dr. Erich Klinger at the University of Minnesota, as quoted in Haddon W. Robinson, *Decision Making by the*

Book (Grand Rapids, MI: Discovery House, 1998), 150.

CHAPTER 2
WHAT ABOUT MY MANGOS?

1. Hank Hanegraaff, "Sickness, Suffering, and the Sovereignty of God," (2000), tape C173.
2. Charnock, *The Existence and Attributes of God,* 490.
3. This was a question posed and answered by Charnock, *The Existence and Attributes of God,* 484.
4. Ibid.

CHAPTER 3
QUESTIONING THE WHIRLWIND

1. Charnock, *The Existence and Attributes of God,* 719.
2. Though parts of this book will dip into such critical issues as miracles, suffering, God's will, and his guidance, I want to assure you that they all are covered in depth in other books in this series. For now, I'd like to concentrate on one important tool that God uses in his providential control of the universe.
3. For more information, read Ali Ahmed and Trygve Tollefsbol, "Telomeres and Telomerase: Basic Science Implications for Aging," *Journal of the American Geriatrics Society,* 49 (2001): 1105–09.
4. God actually used earthquakes in the Old Testament for his special purposes, such as when he sent an earthquake to panic the Philistines (1 Sam. 14:15).
5. Allen P. Ross, "Genesis," in John F. Walvoord, Roy B. Zuck, eds., *The Bible Knowledge Commentary: An exposition of the Scriptures by Dallas Seminary Faculty, Old Testament* (Wheaton, IL: Victor Books, 1985), 33.

6. I cannot say this with absolute certainty because I do not know the mind of God.
7. It is true that the guilt induced by these sins can predispose one to sickness and disease, as is covered in more detail in *Does God Still Do Miracles?* But again, this is just another natural consequence arising from our immoral actions.
8. Dr. Ariel Cohen, *CNN Headline News,* CNN, February 10, 2002.
9. *CNN Headline News,* CNN, December 15, 2001.
10. Peter Kopp and J. Larry Jameson, ed., "Transmission of Human Genetic Disease," *Principles of Molecular Medicine* (Totowa, NJ: Humana Press Inc., 1998), 43.
11. Philip J. Asherson and Sarah Curran, "Approaches to gene mapping in complex disorders and their application in child psychiatry and psychology," *British Journal of Psychiatry,* 179 (2001): 122–28.
12. D. H. Lea, "A clinician's primer in human genetics: what nurses need to know," *The Nursing Clinics of North America,* 35 (2000): 583–614.
13. For an explanation of Romans 8:2, "Because through Christ Jesus the law of the Spirit of life set me free from the law of sin and death," see appendix: "Set Free?"
14. James Dobson, *When God Doesn't Make Sense* (Wheaton, IL: Tyndale House Publishers, 1993), 181.
15. C. S. Lewis, *The Problem of Pain* (New York: Touchstone Books, 1996), 79.
16. Charles Stanley, *How to Handle Adversity* (New York: Inspirational Press, 1995), 202.
17. Jeff Anderson, *Restoring Children of the Streets* (Action International Ministries, 2001), Appendix 1 and 2, http://www.actionintl.org/. Action International is an interdenominational,

Christ-centered organization, a member of the Evangelical Fellowship of Mission Agencies, with offices located in Canada, U.S.A., U.K., and N.Z.

18. (A) Jon Jeter, "Famine Sweeps Southern Africa; Millions Suffering in Crisis Created by Nature, Exacerbated by Man," *The Washington Post,* May 10, 2002, News section. (B) Nicole Itano, "Man-made food crisis grips Southern Africa," *The Christian Science Monitor,* May 15, 2002, News section. (C) "Zimbabwe turns away U.S. food consignment," *AP Worldstream,* May 31, 2002. (D) "World losing war against hunger, says U.N. agency," *The Toronto Star,* June 7, 2002, News section. (E) Karen MacGregor and Katherine Butler, "Once again, African children are dying of hunger. But why is famine afflicting places of such natural wealth?" *Independent,* June 7, 2002, News section. (F) Anneke Van Woudenberg, "Africa at the Crossroads," *Africa News Service,* May 15, 2002.

CHAPTER 4
SPILLING THE GOODS ON EVIL

1. *Rolling Stone,* November 30, 1989, quoted at http://creativequotations.com/one/2599.htm, (accessed April 20, 2005).
2. Ross, "Genesis," 36.
3. Ali Ahmed and Trygve Tollefsbol, "Telomeres and Telomerase: Basic Science Implications for Aging."
4. Amy Ellis Nutt, "No More Growing Old," *Reader's Digest* (Canadian edition), September 2004, 91–95.
5. John MacArthur, "Biblical Perspective on Death, Terrorism, & The Middle East," *Grace to You Ministries,* (2001), tape GC 80-240.
6. Henry T. Sell, as quoted in Donald K.

Campbell, "Joshua," John F. Walvoord, Roy B. Zuck, eds., *The Bible Knowledge Commentary: An exposition of the Scriptures by Dallas Seminary Faculty, Old Testament,* 355.

7. David Olive, "Long list of resume liars bounced from businesses," *The Toronto Star,* October 9, 2002.
8. Paul E. Little, *Know Why You Believe* (Wheaton, IL: Scripture Press Publications, 1967), 78.
9. Little, *Know Why You Believe,* 74.
10. D. Michael Lindsay, "Youth on the Edge: A Profile of American Teens (Results of a Gallup Youth Survey)," *The Christian Century,* October 4, 2003.
11. "Alcohol kills 1,400 students a year," MSNBC, April 9, 2002, http://www.leadingindicators.com/html.lib/newsletter/FYI_02_0410.html, (accessed March 5, 2003).
12. Philip Yancey, *Reaching for the Invisible God* (Grand Rapids, MI: Zondervan, 2000), 56.
13. Based on an Ipsos-Reid poll (2003) as quoted in Gabrielle Bauer, "God & Other Mysteries," *Reader's Digest* (Canadian edition), November, 2003, 50–59.
14. *Xinhua News Agency* (Beijing), "Disasters Hit Asia Most Frequently," March 21, 2002, (data taken from the World Meteorological Organization).
15. *1996 Demographic Yearbook,* New York, United Nations, 1998.

CHAPTER 5
WHERE WAS GOD
ON SEPTEMBER 11?

1. Joke submitted by Terry Tubman on December 9, 2001, to the Web site, http://humor.catweasel.org/Site1/Digests/H0112090.php, Joke 13, (accessed March 11, 2003).

2. As heard on Hank Hanegraaff's radio broadcast, *The Top 10 Outrages of 2002* CD 670, Part A, 2003.

3. The terrorists, in all likelihood, did not expect to bring down each tower with only one airplane. Had their primary goal been to kill as many people as possible, they would have sent all four planes into the Twin Towers in an attempt to collapse the structures quickly.

4. "U.S. carriers reduce flight delays," *Airline Industry Information*, February 4, 2003; Leslie Miller, "Major airlines' performance improved in '02," *AP Worldstream*, February 3, 2003.

5. John MacArthur, *Terrorism, Jihad, and the Bible* (Nashville: W Publishing Group, 2001), 74.

6. The NIV Bible reads, "Because of these, the wrath of God is coming" (Col. 3:6). However, the verb "come," *erchomai*, is present tense and is literally "comes." God's wrath is presently on those who are disobedient.

7. Anne Graham Lotz, interviewed by Jane Clayson, "Where is God," September 13, 2001, http://www.cbs news.com/earlyshow/healthwatch/heal thnews/20010913terror_spiritual.sht ml, (accessed March 5, 2003).

8. Nancy Ellen Hird, "The Church's Secret Shame: Why so many pro-life Christians are getting abortions," *Christian Reader*, July/August 2002, 55.

9. MacArthur, "Biblical Perspective on Death, Terrorism, & The Middle East."

10. Ibid.

11. Ibid.

12. The Minnesota Crime Commission released a report that stated the following: "Every baby starts life as a little savage. He is completely selfish and self-centered. He wants what he wants when he wants it.... Deny him these wants, and he seethes with rage and aggressiveness, which would be murderous, were he not so helpless. He is dirty. He has no morals, no knowledge, no skills. This means that all children, not just certain children, are born delinquent. If permitted to continue in the self-centered world of his infancy, given free reign to his impulsive actions to satisfy his wants, every child would grow up a criminal, a thief, a killer, a rapist." As quoted in Haddon W. Robinson, *Biblical Preaching* (Grand Rapids, MI: Baker Book House, 1980), 145.

CHAPTER 6
HURRICANE KATRINA: GOD'S DIVINE AGENDA?

1. Nancy Gibbs, "An American Tragedy," *Time* magazine (Canadian edition), September 12, 2005, 10–27.

2. John MacArthur, "Spiritual Questions in the Wake of Hurricane Katrina," tape GTY-97, September 6, 2005.

3. Most attribute this quote to Sir Winston Churchill.

CHAPTER 7
THE TOUGHEST QUESTIONS ABOUT GOD

1. Yancey, *Reaching for the Invisible God*, 223.

2. David K. Lowery, "1 Corinthians," in John F. Walvoord, Roy B. Zuck, eds., *The Bible Knowledge Commentary: An exposition of the Scriptures by Dallas Seminary Faculty, New Testament Ed.* (Wheaton, IL: Victor Books, 1983), 510.

3. Carl Stecher, "Looking for God in all the wrong places (Exploring the

Humanist Philosophy)," *The Humanist*, 58 (May 15, 1998): 25.

4. John MacArthur, "Is Israel's Unbelief Inconsistent with God's Plan? Part 3" *Grace To You Ministries*, (1984), tape GC 45-73.

5. As quoted in an interview with Lee Strobel, *The Case For Faith* (Grand Rapids, MI: Zondervan, 2000), 38.

6. As quoted in Gerard Reed, *C. S. Lewis and the Bright Shadow of Holiness* (Kansas City, MO: Beacon Hill Press, 1999), 49.

7. Norman L. Geisler and Paul D. Feinberg, *Introduction to Philosophy: A Christian Perspective* (Grand Rapids, MI: Baker Book House, 1987), 326–27.

8. Ibid., 325, 328.

9. Gerard Reed, *C. S. Lewis and the Bright Shadow of Holiness*, 45.

10. Admittedly in the tribulation period there will be some believers saved who will see God's wrath and power displayed—unlike anything ever witnessed before in history.

11. "Jesus Christ is the same yesterday and today and forever" (Heb. 13:8). It is true that the nature of God never changes, but it is clear from Scripture that God's actions and ways in dealing with mankind have changed over the millennia.

12. Martin Luther King, Jr., "The I Have a Dream Speech," U.S. Constitution Online, http://www.usconstitution. net/dream.html.

13. Mind you, God often does protect the disadvantaged on earth from wicked individuals (see Ps. 12:5).

14. Stephen Charnock, *The Existence and Attributes of God*, 540.

15. Ibid., 508.

16. Ibid., 293.

17. John D. Hannah, "Exodus," in John F. Walvoord, Roy B. Zuck, eds., *The Bible Knowledge Commentary: An exposition of the Scriptures by Dallas Seminary Faculty, Old Testament* (Wheaton, IL: Victor Books, 1985), 123, 125.

18. Charnock, *The Existence and Attributes of God*, 293.

19. As quoted by A. Duane Litfin, "1 Timothy," in John F. Walvoord, Roy B. Zuck, eds., *The Bible Knowledge Commentary: An exposition of the Scriptures by Dallas Seminary Faculty, New Testament Ed.* (Wheaton, IL: Victor Books, 1983), 733.

20. Strobel, *The Case for Faith*, 254.

21. Strobel, in *The Case For Faith*, 255, confessed that prior to his conversion, "I was too proud to bend the knee to anyone, and too enmeshed in my immoral lifestyle to want to give it up."

22. I admit that God chose us first from his perspective (John 6:65; Eph. 1:4).

23. Charnock, *The Existence and Attributes of God*, 603.

24. Ibid., 604.

25. Like most Christians, I believe that children who die before the age of accountability will go to heaven. But the reason they die is because of Adam and Eve's original sin—which has made possible the opportunity for God to display all of his marvelous perfections down through history; something that could not have happened had he sent the human race straight to heaven.

26. Harold Kushner, *Who Needs God?* (New York: Pocket Books, 1991), 196.

27. Ibid.

28. Emily Dickinson, "Truth—is as old as God—," Wikisource, http://en.wikisource.org/wiki/Truth_--_is_as_old_as_God_--.

29. Little, *Know Why You Believe*, 82.

30. Michael Wolff and Ted Koppel, "The Hajj," *ABC Nightline,* ABC, April 18, 1997.

31. Ravi Zacharias, *Jesus Among Other Gods* (Nashville: W Publishing Group, 2000), 6.

32. Ibid., 7.

33. Jeffery L. Sheler, et al., "Faith in America," *U.S. News & World Report,* May 6, 2002, 40.

34. Those who proclaim that there are no absolutes in life (no absolute truth) are contradicting themselves, for they have just made a statement, that if true, must be absolute truth.

35. John MacArthur, *Grace To You* (Panorama City, CA: Grace To You, March 15, 2002).

36. http://www.swedenborg.org/history. cfm.

37. Timothy J. Keller, "Search For God: When All You've Ever Wanted Isn't Enough," tape 234, side B, (New York: Redeemer Presbyterian Church, October 4, 1998).

CHAPTER 8
SOLOMON'S CLUES

1. Most people think they can achieve true happiness and real contentment by way of their "do-it-yourself spirituality." (Mark Galli, managing editor of *Christianity Today*, labels it "Lone-ranger spirituality.")

2. Piper, *Desiring God*, 75.

3. Researchers White and Hatcher conclude, "Clinical studies available indicate that similarity is associated with marital success and is less associated with marital instability and divorce. Evidence suggests that dissimilarity per se is associated with instability and divorce." As cited at http://www.frontline.to/ teaching/dat-

ing_marriage_part2.pdf, (accessed March 5, 2003).

4. Gary Smalley, *Secrets to Lasting Love: Uncovering the Keys to Life-Long Intimacy* (New York: Simon & Schuster, 2000).

5. Ibid., front flap.

6. Ibid., 241–42.

7. Ibid., 135.

8. Ibid., 140. (Smalley is speaking here particularly of the marriage relationship, but the same can be said for many spiritual seekers.)

9. Ibid., 147. (Smalley is talking about a marriage relationship here, but it also applies to our relationship with God.)

10. Ibid., 128.

11. Ibid., 124 (emphasis in original).

12. As quoted in Gary Smalley, *Secrets to Lasting Love,* 124.

13. Ibid., front flap.

14. Ibid., 130.

15. Paul Johnson, *The Quest for God* (Great Britain: Weidenfeld & Nicolson, Orion House, 1996; New York: Harper Perennial, 1997), 171.

16. Timothy J. Keller, "Second Lost Son (And The Dance Of God)," tape 216, side B, (New York: Redeemer Presbyterian Church, January 25, 1998).

17. Ibid.

18. Timothy J. Keller, "Search for Pleasure: When All You've Ever Wanted Isn't Enough," tape 233, side B, (New York: Redeemer Presbyterian Church, September 20, 1998).

19. George Butcher, (sermon, L'Amable Bible Chapel, August 21, 2001).

20. This is the league formally known as "Tier II Junior A." It is not the OHL (Ontario Hockey League).

21. Roy B. Zuck, "Job" in John F. Walvoord, Roy B. Zuck, eds., *The Bible Knowledge Commentary: An exposition of the Scriptures by Dallas Seminary Faculty, Old Testament*

(Wheaton, IL: Victor Books, 1985), 776.

22. J. I. Packer, *Concise Theology: A Guide to Historic Christian Beliefs* (Wheaton, IL: Tyndale House Publishers, 1995), Logos e-book.

23. Ibid.

24. As powerful as these emotions and experiences may be, they are not independent of God's Word. After the risen Lord had appeared to two followers on the road to Emmaus, the men turned to each other and asked, "Were not our hearts burning within us while he talked with us on the road and opened the Scriptures to us?" (Luke 24:32).

25. Piper, *Desiring God*, 76.

26. J. I. Packer, *Knowing God* (Downers Grove, IL: InterVarsity, 1975), 35.